The Tiger in the lard

PTSD and My Journey as a Sexual Abuse Survivor

Barbara Weber PhD

Black Rose Writing | Texas

The author grants the final approval for this literary material.

First printing

This is a work of fiction. Names, characters, businesses, places, events, and incidents are either the products of the author's imagination or used in a fictitious manner. Any resemblance to actual persons, living or dead, or actual events is purely coincidental.

ISBN: 978-1-68433-187-1
PUBLISHED BY BLACK ROSE WRITING
www.blackrosewriting.com

Printed in the United States of America
Suggested Retail Price (SRP) $15.95

The Tiger in the Yard is printed in Garamond

In Memory of those who took their own life as a result of PTSD depression.

A special thank you to all who have been there for me throughout my life. To my husband, Paul, for continuing to be my best friend, love of my life and for putting up with PTSD episodes. To all of the caring adults who have helped me as a child, through adolescence, college, divorce and remarriage and the medical practitioners and therapists who continue to work with me on my continuing struggle.

Thank you to Green Gables photography for my author's photo and I stock photo for the cover photo. my editor Martin Matthews for his expertise, suggestions and patience and to Dr. Shawn Horn for the review. Most of the names in this book are changed.

The Tiger in the Yard

Contents

Forward

At this momentous time, People are bravely and courageously speaking out and telling their stories of abuse and trauma. Historically, when individuals brought their victimization forward it was met with shame, rejection, further abuse, public humiliation and stigmas. Unfortunately, such responses perpetuated the silencing of victims. When we remain silent there is no healing. It is through sharing our stories that not only do we heal, but others heal too. In this book, Dr. Weber, shares her story of childhood abuse, PTSD, her journey in recovery and her victory in healing. She describes the impact of abuse on our lives, relationships and body and describes both PTSD and Complex Trauma disorders. Through her journey of recovery she is now able to say she is healed and no longer meets the diagnostic criteria for PTSD. I applaud Dr. Weber for courageously sharing her story in effort to inspire others to begin their journey in recovery and breaking the "keep the secret" mentality. With this book and the right help, one can begin the journey of healing, have greater self-understanding, self-compassion and ultimately, self-love. It is time we talk about women victimization. Although our stories may be different, they are also the same. Together we can, together we will!

Dr. Shawn Horn, Licensed Clinical Psychologist

A Tiger in the Yard

A picture painted from the center of my being
Symbolizes fear, pain, anger, and defeat:
A slow destruction of a beautiful child.
The Middle-America house looks secure.
Beware the Tiger crouches near.

A troubled child sitting by an empty window
Is stamped upon, trod upon, scratched and marred.
She smells the Tiger's hot, stinking breath
She knows of its trickery
The Tiger lurks near; can anyone hear?

Her yellow tricycle and red wagon litter the front yard.
There, behind the wagon, the Tiger stalks
No one sees the Tiger,
No one knows the dark secrets kept within.
No one cares.

A Guardian

In the 1960s, I was an idealistic hippy who decided that money wasn't important. I wanted to make my little niche of the world better. No matter how or when I died, I wanted to be able to say that everyone I had interacted with was positively influenced and impacted by our interaction. I think I have lived up to that motto. As a result, I am not afraid to speak up when I see what I believe is an injustice or predicament needing action. When I see someone being hurt I do something to stop it because no one stopped my hurt. My experiences venture from getting into a driverless moving car and stopping it to facing a young man holding a gun. We all weave our own tapestry in life. Mine is not a simple weave. Although impacted by my abuse, my life consists of much more.

As a life-long educator, I have worked with children, parents, and teachers. I have taught pre-school, elementary, gifted-pull out, teacher extended education, community college, and university. When teaching in an elementary school, I was walking from my classroom one morning and noticed the principal ahead of me in the parking lot. She was heading into the office. Her car was moving and heading toward me as I walked down the sidewalk. Apparently, she didn't set the brake, and the car was rolling down an incline. I ran to the car, opened the driver's door, hopped in and stopped it. Some may think that is ridiculous. Others may think that it placed me in danger. To me, it was what I do. In my long life, I have done more than just stop a car.

I have confronted bullies, filed suspected child abuse reports, and have faced a man with a gun. My husband was furious; I didn't see any danger in the confrontation.

The first time I spoke up in public for a child was at Disneyland. After I divorced my first husband, I took my young children for a day at the Magic Kingdom. We were standing in line for the Dumbo ride. In front of me were two women in their twenties and a young boy (about seven years old). The women were terrorizing the boy.

The boy was standing quietly. He wasn't running around, he wasn't screaming, he was just standing there.

The older woman said, "I am going to take you back to the car and leave you. Then we will come back and have a good time."

Crying, "No, I don't want to go back to car."

Laughing, "You don't deserve to be here." Their laughter at this child's upset indicated to me that they enjoyed torturing this child.

After a few minutes of this, my children reacted to this meanness. They started to fidget, and both hid behind me. It was as if they were trying to get away from the badgering going on in front of me.

Hesitantly, I said, "What you are doing to this child is horrible." With more confidence, I added, "He isn't doing anything wrong. You need to take some parenting classes." For the rest of the time we were in line, the women stopped talking, which ended their bullying. I never saw them again as we made our way around Fantasyland.

California law states that anyone who is a teacher is required to report suspected child abuse. Spending years in the field, I did just that. I think if it weren't law, I would still report incidents. My own abuse experience causes me to be hypervigilant when it comes to the safety of children.

When teaching first grade, a six-year-old boy came in with abrasions all over his face. I asked him what happened. His response was that his father thinks it funny to step on the front of his skateboard while he was riding it. This stopped the skateboard, and he went flying and landed on his face. This seemed too farfetched for him to make up. After speaking with him for a while, I filled out the paperwork for child protective services.

In our district, I was required to discuss the report with the principal and have him sign off on it before sending it in. The next day, his father barged into the school office waving a gun looking for the person who contacted Child Protective Services. The Principal intercepted him and stopped him at the office. He told me later of the confrontation.

My classroom door opened to the outside (most California elementary schools do not have hallways). Fortunately, he had no idea where his son's classroom was.

My second husband, Paul, called the police and told them they had better keep me safe and keep the man from the school campus until he settled down. Apparently, if the parent has a good lawyer, they can find out who filled out the paperwork for the report to child protective services.

I never heard anything again from this parent.

．　　　．　　　．　　　．　　　．

When my children were six and eight, I remarried. Paul and I took the kids to the local park for a picnic. It was a warm Southern California day, so a lot of families were sitting around a grassy area eating lunch. Not far from us was a big, heavy man, his wife (wearing scrubs, she probably worked at the hospital nearby), and a little boy about five.

I couldn't hear the entire conversation, but I could tell the man was bullying the boy. He raised his voice loud enough for everyone to hear that he would take his belt off and whip him in front of everyone The bullying went on for several minutes. The little boy was so upset he wet his pants. My daughter asked if we could move. My son stopped eating.

"I can't take this anymore," I said, and I got up. Paul remarked, "He is bigger than me." I walked past the family making sure that they noticed that I was watching. Fifty feet away there was a bathroom and around the corner from the building was the ranger station. I opened the door and reported what I saw to the two rangers. They called the authorities and headed out the door to the grassy picnic area.

I went to the bathroom. When finished, the woman in her scrubs passed me. She stopped and looked at me. I thought she was going to be angry. Later, I realized that she was asking for my help. I regret to this day that I didn't ask her if she needed help or at least talk with her. By the time I walked back to where my children were, the family was gone.

Minutes passed, and the ranger came up to me and told me that the police found the family walking home. They were familiar with the family. At this point, domestic violence suspects were not arrested unless the victim pressed charges. I am happy that the police no longer have to wait until charges are filed to act on suspected domestic violence.

．　　　．　　　．　　　．　　　．

Barbara Weber 13

While working in my classroom one day after school, there was a knock on the door. I answered. A woman stood there with two children and a big yellow lab.

"It is hot outside, and we are living in our van. Can we come in and cool off? We will be quiet and not disturb you."

"Sure," I said. "You can put the dog in the fenced in yard. There is a bowl over there for water."

As the woman took the dog to the yard, I asked her children if they wanted to color. They nodded, and I brought out crayons and paper.

Noticing her son's black eye, I asked how he got it.

"He was playing with the dog in the van," the woman said.

I gave her a knowing look that said, "I know he didn't get that playing with the dog." He had no other marks on his face.

I figured I would start a conversation with her.

"You know, when I was a single parent, my husband abused my son. I had to hide him at a friend's house until the case was resolved. I was told that if I didn't make sure that my son was safe, I could lose my children."

"We are living in the van. I just enrolled my children here at this school."

"There are places where you can go where you all will be safe. I would be happy to give you the phone number. It is your choice. I must go to the office to get the phone number. I will be right back."

Upon returning, I said, "If you want to keep your children safe and if you want to keep your children, I would call. They will tell you where to go, and no one can find out where you are." I handed her the phone number. "I need to leave now. Will you be ok?"

She mumbled in hesitation, "Yes."

I locked up my classroom and walked out to my car. Her van was still parked on the street outside of my classroom when I drove away.

The next day, a man barged into the office screaming and shouting. "Where are my children? I am their father. You can't hide them from me." The principal said he had no idea where the children were. They didn't come to school that day.

I was elated. She did take my advice and called the domestic violence hotline.

●   ●   ●   ●   ●

While living in Alaska, we were camping on the Kenai and heard gunshots. The man camping next to us came over and asked us if we knew what was going on. A bullet just whizzed by his head.

Paul took off down a path until he reached a parking lot. He quickly came back to get his phone. "Some guy is target shooting."

I took off down the path through the trees to the parking lot. Paul followed talking on the phone to the police. When I came out of the woods, I saw a young man with his two small children shooting his gun toward a target that was in a direct line with the campground. In my most authoritative mother/teacher voice, I said, "What the hell are you doing? Campers are behind your target. You almost hit a man."

"I'm sorry ma'am. Very sorry." He turned, put his children in the truck, and left.

"Barbara, that man had a loaded gun in one hand and a beer in the other. What were you thinking?"

"I didn't sense any danger. He left, didn't he?"

A little while later, police arrived and took information from Paul. I went back to the camper to sit in the sun and enjoy the rest of the day.

Barbara Weber   15

Father-in-law

I could help strangers. I couldn't help my father-in-law. He remarried shortly after his first wife died. In the following six years, David, my father-in-law, went from a healthy senior who ministered to a small country church every Sunday, walked his dog daily, and looked after his garden, to a frail, thin man with no diagnosis of any major disease. His second wife, Olivia, took him to many different doctors complaining about various "medical problems" that he was experiencing. There was no coordination between doctors, so David was put on a lot of different medications for "problems" that Olivia thought he had. He soon lost weight and was unable to preach or walk his dog.

We visited him about four months before he died. He was on oxygen full-time and was very thin. He was completely dependent upon Olivia for his care. Dinner consisted of a couple cans of Campbell's soup for all of us. Paul made the comment that soup was not enough for dinner, so he scrambled some eggs. Olivia was not thin and looked like she ate well.

As we walked out the door to head home, David said, "This is the last time I will see you." We had to drive the 1300 miles to our home, so we spent the time talking about what we saw and what we didn't see. Both of us thought that he was being abused or maltreated, but it was more of a feeling than being able to pinpoint what exactly was wrong.

Upon arriving home, we called Elder Abuse for their small city. We told them what we felt, the general context that he went from healthy to frail in a few short years and yet did not have a diagnosable disease. They visited the home and spoke with David. Of course, he said everything was fine. Paul thinks he was too embarrassed to speak about what was going on. They didn't see any outward signs of abuse, so they closed the case.

We got a call from Paul's sister, Amy, the day David was sent to the hospital and put into ICU. She told Paul that Olivia had signed paperwork that none of

David's children could find out anything about David's condition.

Paul said something about getting a court order to find out what is wrong. Amy remarked, "There isn't any time. I will get the records. I know how to do that. Also, Olivia has asked that the body be cremated. I want an autopsy. You should see him. It looks to me like he was beaten. He has blood, cuts, and bruises all over his head. I will call you back."

Paul agreed. "Keep me posted."

Amy asked the doctor what had happened to David and he told her that apparently, he had fallen off the toilet. She spent a little time speaking with the doctor. When they finished the conversation, he told her to wait a minute that he would be back. When he came back, he had a folder and a piece of paper for her to sign requesting an autopsy. She signed it and handed it back to him. He thanked her, turned around and left. The folder was still on the counter. The doctor must have left it accidentally. Amy picked it up and put it into her purse.

David died that afternoon. Amy called the Rangers. She dropped by the station and told them that she thought David was murdered. After hearing her story and looking at the medical records, the Rangers picked Olivia up and took her in for questioning. They also went back to the house with Amy and cut out the huge hole in the wall.

Sheetrock is difficult to break. David weighed less than one hundred pounds. The forensics personnel stated that they felt it would be unlikely that someone weighing less than one-hundred pounds could fall off the toilet and create such a huge hole in the wall. Amy thought he was thrown into the wall.

Two days after his death, Olivia had items that she wanted to keep moved and an auction company took what she didn't want. She had a salvage company come in and remove anything else left in the house. By the time of the funeral, the house was completely empty.

David and Paul's mother, Beatrice, had purchased a house in a Christian retirement neighborhood set up so if one or both owners need assisted living or nursing care (the facilities are in the community) it would be provided free of charge. Paul's mother had lupus. She used the nursing home during her last few months of life.

When Paul and I visited before David's death, I said something about Olivia staying on after David died. Apparently, she didn't think about that. They looked up the rules. The only person allowed to stay in the house after David's death was

Beatrice.

Olivia had no claim to the house. We think that is why the will was changed to leave everything else to Olivia.

Paul flew down for the funeral. His brother, Amy, and sister were not allowed anywhere near the house. Olivia's son guaranteed that. Paul found out to his surprise that he was no longer executive of the estate.

Upon further review, Paul felt strongly that his father didn't sign it. During the years, David had changed his wills many times. Each time, he sent a copy to his children, Paul, Amy, Abbey, and Brian. Each will was signed David Weber. The will written two months before his death was signed with initials only. David's children were left out of the will. There was no division of the monetary or physical assets. Everything went to Olivia.

David was a WWII veteran, and he had asked for a military funeral. It didn't happen, and Paul did not receive the traditional American flag. The funeral was held in the church social hall. Paul and Amy were specifically told that they couldn't speak. But then, Paul and Amy don't always follow instructions. Paul got to speak. He wanted to say that he thought Olivia had killed his dad but opted instead to state that he had been healthy and deteriorated quickly in the past five years. He stopped just short of accusing Olivia.

It was not a good day for any of Paul and his siblings. They were dealing with their own grief and felt strongly that David was helped to an early death.

After the funeral, Amy went home and searched the internet. Even though Amy was adopted, she and her sister Abbey were raised by David and Beatrice (David's first wife). They were Mom and Dad to her. Both Amy and Abbey were taken from their biological parents by child protective services when Amy was four and Abbey was two. Their parents were drug addicts and would open the house to friends to party. As a group, they would take turns sexually molesting both girls.

A few days after the funeral, the first bit of information Amy found was that Olivia had been married five times. Each time her husband was healthy at the time of marriage and died within a few years. She called me immediately.

She then took that information to the Rangers. They went back to the house to see if they could find anything and there was nothing there. Everything in the house was gone. We believed that he died from ingesting one of the landscape products that he used when he would garden. There was no hope of finding any gardening products.

David's autopsy showed nothing. Tests for poison were negative. There was nothing but head trauma but that could have happened when he "fell off the toilet." She felt strongly that David's health had been systematically and deliberately undermined and that Olivia had thrown him off the toilet resulting in the hole in the wall. Proving it was another thing.

Amy was tenacious. She looked at the obituaries for all of Olivia's previous husbands. Her first husband was ill for several weeks (according to the story Olivia told), he looked terrible, was grey in color and in bed before passing away. The coroner told her that in the 1950s and '60s when a young man died, they didn't do an autopsy, they wrote heart attack on the death certificate as a common practice. No autopsy was conducted.

Her second husband also died within five years of marriage to Olivia. He was cremated immediately after death. We couldn't locate any relatives for him.

Olivia's third husband was disabled and needed a wheelchair to get around. Amy spoke with his brother. He told her that Olivia and his brother had been married a short time. Apparently, Olivia physically abused him. He called his brother for help, and he drove from Colorado to Texas to pick him up. That was Olivia's only divorce.

I spoke with the brother of her fourth husband. The first words out of his mouth when I asked him about Olivia were, "She is a Black Widow."

He told me that his brother was healthy when he married her, and within five years, he was dead. His body was cremated.

We hoped that the Rangers would investigate and acquire enough information to obtain a court order to exhume Olivia's first husband. When a young man died in the '50s or '60s, heart attack was the reason given for death even though the person may not have died of a heart attack. The Medical Examiner in Dallas, where Olivia's first husband died, wanted to do an autopsy to see exactly how he had died, but since Olivia had control of the body and we didn't have enough evidence to obtain a court order, the body was never exhumed.

In the meantime, the rangers were raiding a religious compound and were investigating the sexual abuse of young girls. All the women and children were removed. Every Ranger was busy on this case. They closed David's case.

Amy wasn't finished, however. She visited Olivia's church a couple of times.

From one of David's wills, she knew that David had given $60,000 to the pastor of the church to invest for him. She wanted to know what happened to the money.

The pastor was no longer at that church. Amy asked the church secretary why. The secretary said that he had embezzled money and no, the church did not file charges. Amy asked about the $60,000 that David gave to the pastor to invest. The secretary told her that the money was gone. David wasn't the only church member who gave the Pastor money to invest.

The sister of the pastor that embezzled money was the lawyer that signed off on the changed will for David. To us, we had uncovered an illegal plan to take money from seniors. However, the Rangers were busy, and all we had was circumstantial evidence. Without a clear-cut method of determining exactly what happened to David that day or to his money, the case was closed. To this day, Paul feels he did not do enough to protect his father. Living over one thousand miles away, I am not sure what more we could have done.

Paul did get some satisfaction. He called the church secretary and obtained information as to where the pastor had moved. The secretary informed him that the Pastor was working at a Christian University and was pastor of a church in California. Paul called the Christian University and the organization overseeing the church and suggested that they contact the church where their new employee was previously a pastor. He told them that the man had embezzled money and taken money from unsuspecting and trusting seniors. He made sure that he told them to check it out and not take his word for it. A few weeks later, Paul got an angry, threatening phone call from the pastor. If we were still in California, Paul said he would have filed for a restraining order.

Paul also contacted the organization that ordains pastors. He is not sure if the pastor lost his credentials to minister to congregations.

Heartbroken

It was evening. Paul and I were sitting in the family room reading. Vivaldi violin concerto played in the background. The phone rang. Paul got up to answer it.

"Hi, Paul. This is Alan."

"Hey, Alan. How are you?"

"Amy was diagnosed with cancer a few days ago, we are going to Anderson Cancer Institute next week. We are waiting for a call back to tell us the day and time to be there."

"Alan, we are so sorry to hear this. Please tell her that our hearts go out to her and that we love her."

"Will do."

Paul handed me the phone. Alan, we know how difficult this can be and your time spent at Anderson will be very busy but is it possible for you to text an update when you know something. We are concerned. Please tell her that we wish the best for her and we are thinking about her."

"OK, I will send you a text when we find out anything."

"Thank you for letting us know. Bye."

Amy is Paul's younger sister. Even though we live 2000 miles away, we have communicated via phone and SKYPE. We are glad Alan called. Alan and Amy are devoted Christians believing in the Bible as the Word of God. The earth is 6000 years old. Paul and I are completely at the other end of the continuum as far as political and religious beliefs are concerned. However, we were able to find common ground and often spoke on SKYPE.

•   •   •   •   •

One evening I received a text message. It's Alan. "Just got scheduled for Amy's first appointment at MD Anderson this Thursday…heading down to Houston tomorrow. Probably there for at least a week".

He continued, "So far no answers to location of the source of the cancer and hence, no treatment plan. Seems like more biopsies on the horizon."

The next text came from Alan the following day. "We're back home after one day in MD Anderson. We had appointments scheduled for two days, but things didn't work out the way they were planned. The doctors were very helpful and candid about the gravity of the situation. Her time is short. Amy and I now face the decision whether to begin Chemo...thinking always of how best to glorify God in these final days. Of course, we have prayed for healing and know God is working things out for his glory and our good. She has less than six months to live."

"We are sorry to hear this. Is it possible for us to speak with her via the phone or SKYPE? If we can, we want to drive down and say goodbye's, but we don't want to be a burden."

"We began hospice care yesterday. Amy still cannot speak. If you call me, I will help her communicate. Go ahead and call, now is a good time."

"Amy, we just wanted to thank you for all of the work you did after Dad died. You did a lot of work. And we want to tell you how much we love you. Do you color? Many doctors have their patients color because it is supposed to help with pain."

"Yes, she colors."

"Does she color with crayons or colored pencils?"

"She uses colored pencils."

"I will go to Michaels to get a couple of books and a set of pencils. What kind does she like?"

"She likes the Crayola brand."

"Ok, look for the package in about three days."

We talked for a little while longer and said goodbyes. Three weeks later Alan called to tell us that she had passed away that morning. He wanted me to know that she had taken all the pencils I had sent, put them into a large mug, and had them on her table that went over the bed. She colored with them up until the day before she died when her hands were too shaky to hold the pencil.

We were soul sisters. When she was 3 or 4, both she and her younger sister were removed from their parents. The parents were "druggies" and had parties where they allowed the girls to be molested by other party goers. Paul's father and mother adopted both her and her sister.

I too was molested from the age of 5 to the age of 10 by my father. Amy and I broached the subject a couple of times but didn't get into anything other than we had similar histories. I was not removed from the house because the federal government didn't make it mandatory for states to provide protective services until I was 11, almost 12. Amy was 10 years younger than me.

When someone dies, we often think of questions we wished we had asked them. I am no different. I wish I had asked Amy if she had PTSD, flashbacks, walked in her sleep, woke up screaming at night from nightmares and wanted to take her own life. Afraid to raise a sensitive subject, I never asked her.

Childhood sexual abuse is the secret that no one talks about. Women who speak up as adults who have been victimized are more than likely considered to be lying or trying to make money by bringing their victimization forward. It is time we talk about women victimization. It is time we face the economic and physical toll it places on the victim. I regret not speaking with Amy. I fell into the same "keep the secret" mentality that is commonplace in society today.

PTSD

Crawling into bed,
It is nap time, I am three.
Asleep, the bedroom door slams on my hand,
The room spins. I scream.
Every night, the hand is slammed,
The room spins, I no longer scream out loud.
At sixteen the spinning stops,
Nightmares continue.

At six, I walk in my sleep. I am still walking.
Waking up in the dark somewhere — terrified!
I continue to walk. Front door is locked
Alarm between bedroom door.

Screaming!
A man standing by the bed — my husband wakes up.
No one is there. I am dreaming.
Years pass. Night terrors continued.

Men chasing me
Over and over, I try to call 911
Can't push correct buttons.
Woke up — phone in hand
No 911 operator answered.

Men chasing, need to hide
Sat down hard on floor, fell back, hit head
Concussion!

Broke hand pounding on bed-end table
Never woke up!

Years of nightly terrors!
Years of waking up screaming!
PTSD

Post-traumatic stress disorder is a life-sized weight that wrapped around my body. It can't be removed, it is always there. Sometimes the weight is overpowering, covering me entirely. Other times its presence is only bothersome. However, at night it sneaks up on me through dreams; terrible, frightening dreams that cause me to walk in my sleep scream loudly, and at times hurt myself.

My PTSD started when I was three years old there was a lot of stress in the household. We lived on sixth street, had chickens in the backyard and slugs in the side yard. Slugs are slimy, ugly brown snails without their shells. My brother would take the slugs and terrorize me by throwing them at me, shoving them in my face and putting them on my clothes. I hated that part of the backyard where they lived. It was dark and wet.

Every Sunday, one of my brothers would go into the yard, grab one chicken at a time, place the chicken on the chopping block and with one movement of the ax, chop the head off. Sometimes, I watched and wondered why the bodies ran around the yard after their heads were removed. I always noticed the blood which ran down the chopping block to the ground. That was my normal.

I have more memories of events that occurred in that house than any other house as a child. I guess I remember them because they are not good memories. At one point, Elmer, (my father) had his mother move in with us. I was always getting into trouble stepping on her feet or bothering her one way or another. I have no idea how long she lived with us, but she was quickly placed into a mental institution (I assume that is where individuals were placed that also had Alzheimer's at that time). We visited her a couple of times, but when it became clear that she didn't remember any of us, we stopped dropping by.

Before Grandma went into the hospital, the stress on my mother, Marie, was evident because she took it out on me. Many yardsticks were broken as they hit my rear, and then fly swatters were used because they didn't break. I probably asked too many questions, wanted to help and needed attention. When my daughter was three, I looked at her development, curiosity, ability to ask a lot of questions and her normal need for attention. I couldn't understand the idea of using corporal punishment. It wasn't necessary at all.

It was at this time (three-years-old) that my PTSD started. Marie would put me down to take a nap. I saw my hand slammed in the bedroom door, the room started to spin. With each passing second, it gained momentum, whirling faster and faster. Screaming got my mother's attention. She came into the room and angrily told me that my hand wasn't in the door and to go back to sleep. That didn't stop the room from spiraling, it didn't stop me from being frightened or "seeing" my hand still caught in the door. Eventually, the spinning stopped, and I was able to go back to sleep.

After experiencing this horrifying experience a few times, I stopped shouting for my mother. This image along with the spinning room lasted until I was sixteen, and I was able to somehow get the room to stop its oscillation. To this day, I have no idea how I stopped the room from spinning. The whirling bedroom morphed into different nightmares.

Charlotte, my therapist, thought I had been sexually abused from the time I was three. I don't remember what trauma happened to me before I started seeing my hand in the door. When four, I remember wetting my pants and coming home from a friend's house with a doll blanket tucked into my pants so that no one would see. When I mentioned that, Charlotte was convinced that my abuse started when I was three.

Regardless of the trauma, individuals that have PTSD have common symptoms. I am no different. I have walked in my sleep since I was at least six. My mother told me that she would see me walk out of my room and would tell me to go back to bed. At that point, I would turn around and go back to bed. I never remembered anything about walking around at night unless I woke up not knowing where I was, or I woke up because I hurt myself.

Sometimes, I would wake up in the dark and not know where I was. Intensely frightened, stumbling around, I eventually found some furniture or some other item that helped me determined where I was. Eventually, I would find a door or a light switch, turn the light on and could find my way back to bed. Waking up terrified has been a way of life for me since I was three.

As an adult, whenever I had a new primary physician, I would mention my sleepwalking and dreams. I always got the same comment: "Just make sure you are safe, keep the front door locked so you don't go outside." In Alaska and Wyoming, the danger was greater. Walking outside in the winter at -20 degrees would be deadly!

I had difficulty sleeping. I often sat up, talked, and fumbled with items on the table next to my bed. Sometimes, I woke my husband, and sometimes I woke myself up. Words such as disturbing, terrorizing, frightening and alarming just don't do my terror justice. I have never been able to sleep without some sort of nightmare on a nightly basis.

I always thought I was just someone who had vivid dreams. I had no idea that what I had experienced my entire life was PTSD until my current primary physician used the term. I always thought that PTSD was what veterans had when they returned from war. I was in therapy in the early '80s, before there was much information about it.

Before and after therapy, I had repeated dreams of a man in my bedroom next to my bed. I could describe him in detail (what he was wearing, what he looked like, how tall he was, etc.) and even if I woke up, I would still insist he was there. It was never the same man. My response was always the same, I woke up screaming, "A man is in the room." Both Abani (my first husband) and Paul would tell me there was no one there. I insisted. Eventually, I woke up enough to realize that there wasn't anyone there and laid down and tried to go back to sleep. Seeing men in my room frightened the hell out of me.

Other than dreams about men in my bedroom, I dreamt that horses were chasing me. They see me and start to run toward me. They are frightening, large, strong and fast. I always wake up before they hurt me; too frightened to stay asleep.

A regular problem in most of my dreams was my attempts to call 911 for help. Every time I tried to call, I press the wrong buttons. No matter how many times I attempted to press the correct buttons, I was never successful.

Undoubtedly the most embarrassing incident occurred when I was dreaming that six Martians were coming to get me. They were green, had a skinny waist, legs and arms and a big round head. I woke up with the phone in my hand that was making a beeping sound. I had tried to call 911 in my sleep. I can't imagine how embarrassed I would have been if the dispatcher had answered and asked me what my emergency was. If I had answered, "Help, green Martians are coming after me!" I am afraid of what the response of the dispatcher would have been.

Several years ago, I was dreaming that men were coming after me. I had to find a place to hide. Walking outside (in my dream), I noticed a corner near the fence that had an aluminum cover over it. As I went to sit down under the cover, I sat down on the floor hard enough to wake me for an instant. I then fell back hit my head on the wall and knocked myself out. I woke up with my dog, Dugga, licking my face. I was slumped forward with my head on the floor. It was dark, and I was alone. I had no idea how long I was knocked out.

Managing to stand up, I figured out I was in my office because my office chair was nearby. Feeling my chair, then my desk and moving to the door, I headed to the bathroom. Paul called out asking me where I was. I told him I was going to the bathroom. I finished and crawled back into bed and said nothing. The next morning, my head felt like it was going to explode, so I went to the ER. I suffered a concussion and ended up spending all week in bed. I couldn't sit up without getting dizzy and nauseated.

Aside from nightmares which are one kind of flashbacks, PTSD is also associated with depression. I have been suicidal several times and think I have had some degree of depression most of my life. After a couple of years in my first marriage, I realized that I had made a huge mistake. I felt trapped and believed that no one cared about me. I knew I cared about no one. One evening after enduring a barrage of criticisms from Abani, I took every pill from a new bottle of both Tylenol (that is all that I had in the medicine cabinet). Nothing happened except that I became very ill.

After I decided to divorce my first husband, at the beginning of my therapy, I thought I was going to be made to go back to him. I became suicidal again. I wrote a suicide note and told my therapist. I had to see her every day for a couple of weeks, and she had my doctor prescribe anti-depressants for me.

•   •   •   •   •

I retired early, and we moved to a state that was just not a good fit for us. I hated it, and within six months, I wanted to move. Paul persuaded me to give it a chance. Two years later, feeling trapped, I was suicidal again. Paul wouldn't leave me alone. No matter where I was, he was not far away. Thinking that rubbing my arms and back would make me feel better that was what he did. He said he didn't know what else to do. After a month or so, I came out of such a deep depression. We decided to put the house on the market. Unfortunately, the recession of 2008 determined that we had to wait for another four years to be able to move. We had to sell our house at a loss, and we moved to another state. We are much happier in this new state.

I don't know what it is about PTSD and suicide. The two are ultimately entwined. I am not certain if it is because old memories are etched into the brain's wiring and are still vivid, or if it is the off and on struggle with sleep disturbance, flashbacks or memory triggers. It just may be the heavyweight of PTSD.

When I was to reaching closure of my abuse, I again was suicidal. This time I had planned to take an overdose of pain medication (I had over 200 extra pills in my cabinet from various surgeries and planned to take them). I thought if I took them at night, I wouldn't wake up. With the help of Paul and my medical doctor, I was able to throw out the pills.

I still fight depression. Even though I have been successful in eliminating the nightmares, triggers, and sleepwalking. I am still in therapy for Complex PTSD criteria including depression. I have always done all the right things to combat mild depression. I enjoy getting out away from the city to camp and hike. Painting allows me to express my innermost feelings and I enjoy sewing. The most powerful depression eliminators are my children and grandchildren. When they visit, my depression disappears.

Regularly and expectantly, I am reminded of something that happened to me long ago. I can also be reminded of a feeling that I had. These are called triggers and have happened periodically over my lifespan. I usually pull into myself and am very quiet. It takes me a while to figure out what the trigger was and what it made me remember. Once I figure that out, I stayed in my cave, so-to-speak, for about three or four months. Paul knows when I have difficulty. He waits patiently for me to 'return to him,' his description for what happens to me after a trigger.

For instance, one year while teaching kindergarten, the Special Education teacher came into my class to teach my children tolerance toward special needs students. She gave each child a mirror and had them draw a straight line, a circle, and finally write their name while looking in the mirror. As expected, the children had a difficult time doing this task. When the special education teacher put tape around one of the children's fingers, I got really upset. I thought it was taking power away from the child and I told her to stop. She did, but it took me several months to get over it.

Complaining to my primary physician that I was having difficulty sleeping, he had me do a sleep study. That required me to sleep one night in a sleep lab. I didn't think anything about having a sleep study until I had to spend it in a room with a male technician down the hall. I was distressed all night. It took me four months to get over it.

Early Years

World War II ended in June of 1945 and started an era of the "perfect" family. Husbands went to work, and their wives stayed home "keeping house," as my mother used to say. When the "breadwinner" came home, he was met by a loving wife, tidy house and newly bathed children busy doing homework or heading to bed. It was an "Ozzie and Harriet" and "Leave It to Beaver" existence. Man was king, and woman was, well...woman was.

Born a year after the end of the war, I am a member of the first year of the Baby Boomer generation. As the second of two girls in the family and along with three boys, there were five children in the family until I was seven, at which time another girl was born. There are four years between my older brother and me, seven years between the youngest child and me. My father, Elmer, was narcissistic, always wanting to be the center of attention, verbally abusive to my mother and manipulative. Most notably, he was a pedophile. My mother, Marie, knew about his abuse of children before he victimized me. I am not sure if she knew he also molested my older sister.

I was born in a Midwest city. At the age of two, the family moved to another Midwest town where Elmer obtained a job as a professor in the theater arts department at the university in town. We also attended the Methodist church where Elmer was an active church member. He even taught Sunday school.

My abuse started when I was in kindergarten. Since kindergarten ended in the middle of the day, I was instructed to walk down the street to the machine shop (where scenery from the Theater Department was created and stored). Elmer was to meet me there to take me home.

It didn't take long for me to walk the short distance to the shop. Sometimes my older brother would put me on his back-bike fender and drop me off. I would sit on the fender. Once I caught my foot in the spokes. From then on, I held my legs far out away from the spokes as we rode down the hill.

My father was always at the door waiting for me, and the machine shop was always empty. Instead of taking me home right away, he took me in the back where all the very large back-drop sets were stored. He took me between the standing backdrops and molested me.

A couple of years later, my mother noticed that I had a quarter and asked where I got it. I told her Elmer gave it to me and what he did to me. When he came home, she screamed and yelled at him creating a disruptive, loud, long and upsetting argument. Unfortunately for me, what she didn't do, was tell him to leave.

I remember the first abuse situation (at 5), the last (at 10) and the time he stuck his penis in my mouth. I was so horrified and repulsed that I think he took it out. I don't remember if he was able to manipulate me into giving him oral sex or not after that.

At ten, my older brother found us naked on the bed in the master bedroom. Upon seeing my brother, Elmer threw me off the bed. Ashamed, I crawled to my bedroom.

My Friends

When I was eight, my oldest brother spent the summer on a fishing boat in the Northwest. I took advantage of his absence and moved all my dolls upstairs to his bedroom. I set up a pretend cabin and placed my dolls in makeshift beds. My dolls were ill or had broken bones. I was a nurse living alone in Alaska; these children were my responsibility. I made splints for broken bones, nursed children with polio, and life-threatening illnesses. My supplies came from my parents' medicine cabinet from which I mixed concoctions to make salves and healing tonics. "Physician, heal thyself" is what I was doing. As I played with my dolls, I listened to a record of the "Nutcracker Suite" the entire time I was playing.

When school started again in the fall, I went back to the university K-12 school. I had been in the school since kindergarten. Children who attended this school had parents who were professors, medical doctors at the university and/or medical school and business professionals in the community.

Most of the girls in my class belonged to Camp Fire Girls. Our leader was the wife of the owner of the sand and gravel pit in the town and mother of one of my best friends, Emily.

In the summer, I would spend a day or two at Emily's house playing with her and swimming in her lake. In the winter, I often went home with her on Fridays and spent the night. We would play dolls, and I remember several times I celebrated Hanukkah with her. As I sat, they would go through the story of the Menorrhea, and when done, Emily would light the candle. I was one of their family.

Visiting Abigail's family was no different. Both of her parents were Ph.Ds teaching in the music department at the university. (Having a mother with a Ph.D. didn't seem strange to me at that time, although I assume it was fairly rare in the 1950s). Abigail and I would play after school, and I always stayed for dinner before they took me home. When I sat down for dinner, next to my plate was a vitamin just like Abigail. I remember a specific time when we were eating T-bone steak. I was having trouble getting all the meat off the bone. I was told, "Just pick it up and eat it." I did! Just like Abigail!

Coming home was the best. We would always get into their car, and if the sun was setting in front of us, and we were on a hill, the special button on the dash was pushed (sometimes they let me push it). The wings came out from underneath the car, and it would take off flying into the sky. (Of course, that was only in our imagination, but it was fun, and we did it every time they drove me home.)

Ava's father owned an electronics store in town and owned a farm where he raised cattle. Ava's mother had a degree in psychology but was losing her sight, so she didn't teach at the university. They also treated me like one of the family. Ava's mother would often show me new kitchen electronics. One visit, she was excited about a new oven that could cook a potato in ten minutes.

One night at dinner, Ava's father was talking excitedly about a new type of steer. I thought that was strange since they had no cattle in their backyard. I thought maybe he worked at the university in the animal husbandry department. After that, I went to the farm with Ava and her family and saw the herd of black cattle.

It never entered my mind that my routine visits to the houses of Emily, Abigail and Ava were anything but elementary school friends inviting friends over to play.

I don't remember inviting anyone over to my house other than for birthdays. I recently connected with a couple of my elementary school friends. In chatting with Abigail, I asked her if she remembered the routine with the car and flying. She said she did. In our conversation, I mentioned being a survivor of childhood sexual abuse. She knew exactly what I was talking about because she is a lawyer, and years ago worked as an advocate for children of sexual abuse.

Apparently at some point, I told Abigail that my father touched me. I don't recall that. She said she didn't quite understand what I meant, so she asked her mother. Her mother gave her some sort of explanation, but Abigail still didn't understand. However, she and I both think that her mother told Emily and Ava's mother what was going on at my house. The summer between second and third grade, Vickie's mother explained to me that Emily sold over one hundred boxes of Camp Fire Girl candy and she managed to send me to camp as well. These mothers guaranteed that I went to camp and was part of stable families throughout my elementary school years. They cared enough about me to make me part of their families.

Abigail also mentioned that she remembered sitting downstairs at my house (it was my birthday, she thought) with all my friends. Elmer started to come down the stairs, and my mother grabbed his arm and stopped him. At the time, she thought it was strange.

She spoke of seeing me at school with swollen eyes, and I often looked like I was ill. Abigail couldn't remember if she said anything to me. She just didn't understand what was going on with me.

Emily grew up to join the Peace Corps and become a state representative. She was on the committee on Violence Against Women. Abigail became a lawyer initially working with children of sexual abuse and turning to Native American issues. Ava became a marriage and family counselor. They all followed their parent's roles as involved and caring individuals.

Elmer decided to move the family to California in the middle of my sixth-grade year. January 1958 was the same year that the social security amendment came into law requiring states to have child protective services. This is just a theory, or maybe it was just a coincidence: I wonder if Abigail's parents said something to Elmer about what he was doing to me. Elmer, worried about the law, packed the family up to move to California. This disrupted all of us. I think my older sister was hurt the most because 1958 was the year she was graduating from a small high school. Extremely shy as she was, it was difficult for her to spend the last half of her senior year in a very large high school in California.

I wish I could have found Abigail years ago. We would have talked, and maybe her parents would still have been alive so that I could speak to them. I have so many questions, and I want to thank them for what they did for me. More importantly, I would tell them that I am all right. With their help, I managed to struggle through my problems and have become a success.

Looking back on the relationship I had with my friends and their families, I think that was a strong reason why I ended up staying in school. Even though I graduated high school in the sixties, I didn't embrace the drug culture, run away from home, and I never had a stint of homelessness. I attribute my ability to stay in school to what my friends' families did for me. For my entire elementary school experience, I was surrounded by caring families.

California

I finished the last semester of my sixth-grade year in a new elementary school. I joined campfire girls and a Methodist youth group. This gave me a core group of friends and surrogate parents who oversaw each group.

I was lucky to have surrogate parents while I traversed the difficult teen years. During seventh and eighth grade, the Methodist Youth Fellowship counselors were a couple with two children. They were positive and offered guidance through various activities.

However, Bill and Doree Post probably made the most positive impact upon me. They were professional gospel writers and singers, yet they made time to be leaders of our MYF group for several years. They wrote *Sixteen Reasons,* sung by Connie Stevens as well as many other contemporary songs during the 1950s and early '60s. Doree died of stomach cancer in 1961. None of us in the MYF knew of her illness until she died. I was in the tenth grade.

Even though I had found a group of friends and had activities outside of school, junior high was boring to me. I was no longer in a class of children from families whose mother and/or father were PhDs or MDs. Even though I was tracked into the highest classes, for the most part, they were uninteresting, and I had trouble adjusting.

I did enjoy my Spanish class and my math class, but in social studies, I played games. I pretended to not understand why I was flunking the tests even though I said that I had studied. That was a lie. I never opened the book. The teacher sent a referral in for the psychologist to give me some tests. I specifically recall the IQ test. Although I answered questions, I sprawled on the table, put my head down and yawned a lot. I remember repeating long number sequences back to the psychologist. When done, I went back to class. Nothing further was done with me regarding any more testing. Back in class, I don't remember if I started reading the material or listening; but I ended up getting a C as a final grade. I suspect that was a gift.

At thirteen, I started my menses. With the limited information that I was given in the sixth-grade class on human development, I didn't understand everything about reproduction. My molestation had stopped when I was ten, yet once I started my menses, I was terrified that I was somehow going to get pregnant.

After several trips to the school nurses' office complaining of illness, the nurse sat me down and spoke to me sternly about coming to her office when there was nothing wrong with me. I wanted to ask her, to tell her, but I couldn't make any sense if I tried. I wanted to tell her that I was afraid. I needed to speak to someone, anyone about my feelings, about my fear of getting pregnant. Maybe to tell her what happened to me. She kept talking. She just went on and on, and on. I sat looking at my cold, shriveled hands in my lap as she bellowed. I left her office never to return.

For the next three years, I worried about pregnancy. It wasn't until I was in tenth-grade biology that I learned that sperm lives three days and that there was no chance that I could get pregnant from the abuse. The relief was enormous!

During the tenth-grade, Elmer was arrested for the attempted molestation of my sister's friend. The six-year-old came to the door to see if my younger sister could play. Apparently, he attempted to molest the little girl. She ran home and told her mother. He was arrested and spent one night in jail.

Within a few days, three men from the college where my father taught came to gather his signature. He was being fired. I ran around the house, laughing and giggling trying to show them what a happy family we were. No one came to talk with us. No one asked my sisters or me if we had been molested. If they had, I would have lied.

When it came time for Elmer to go to court, the little girl couldn't keep her story straight and got confused. (He said she lied). The judge dropped the charges but instructed him to see a psychiatrist. After the visit with the psychiatrist, he came home and proudly announced that there was nothing wrong with him. He didn't have to see the psychiatrist again. I thought that if there is nothing wrong with him, there was a hell of a lot wrong with me.

We had to move. I spent my last two years of high school at a new school and made one close friend, played in the band and was in the debate team. I was quite good at debate and won several awards. Researching the topics for discussion was fun for me.

After I graduated, I went to Valley College (a two-year community college). I didn't realize that I had the ability and grade point average to attend a four-year institution. When I transferred to Cal State Los Angeles (now Cal State University at Los Angeles), I was told that my GPA and SAT scores were high enough to go directly to a university from high school. It was just as well; I didn't have the money to attend a university.

At the four-year university, I had trouble concentrating, so I sought out therapy at the college counselor's office. We worked together to come up with ways for me to improve my concentration. We focused on helping me become a better student. I rewarded myself when I found that I was concentrating on studying. I ate carrot and celery sticks. She also suggested that I take an IQ test. I arranged to take it but never went back for the results. The purpose of the test was to show me that I could do very well in school. She encouraged me to go to Stanford to get my MA and continue to my Ph.D.

After a few visits, she asked me to draw or paint a couple of pictures. The first picture that I drew had daisies with tall stems. Hidden in the daisies, a large skunk sat on its haunches. At some point, I also drew a picture of my family using only pencil. The picture image was of wooden boards standing next to each other.

After showing the counselor the pictures, we got into a conversation, and I finally told her that I was sexually abused as a child. Mentioning that she thought that is what happened, she told me she was waiting for me to come forth and discuss it with her. We didn't concentrate on the sexual abuse.

As we spoke, she got to know me better and said I was very creative. She suggested that I take a couple of art classes. There was a reason why I didn't take any art classes, I told her. In the seventh grade, we were asked to do a book report poster. I did mine on Robinson Crusoe. I painted animals from the story around the poster as a border. No animals were in scale to each other. Some were large, and some were small. The morning that the posters were due, I stood in line outside the classroom waiting for the teacher to open the door. A group of students was talking about the assignment. We all showed our posters to each other. When I showed my poster, it was pointed out that the animals were not in scale with each other. They all laughed and made fun of it. I felt terrible. It didn't make any difference to me that my poster ended up on the wall and that I had received an A. What made the difference to me was that my peers made fun of it and I translated that to me. From then on until I was in college, I took only one class using clay and never did any other art at home or at school.

She convinced me that it was worth a try for me to take just one drawing course. If I didn't like it, I could drop it. Taking her suggestion, I enrolled in a beginning drawing class. It was fun. Drawing with charcoal rather than pencil gave me the freedom to use my fingers and chamois to illustrate light and dark contrast on the newsprint. I really enjoyed it. (I also recognized that artistically, I wasn't too bad.) I kept that artwork for a long time, but unfortunately, it has long since deteriorated.

As I continued to work with the counselor, I learned to concentrate on my studies and ended up on the Dean's list. Which is rather funny. I received notification in the mail that I was on the Dean's list. I went to the ceremony. My name wasn't on the program, so I went up to the podium anyway. I told them that I had received a letter. They said my name wasn't there. I never questioned the status and never picked up the award.

Even though I enjoyed painting, I was happiest when I could sit in the library with books and journals on any topic of my choice surrounding me. I also enjoyed my science classes. Anatomy, physiology, organic chemistry, and microbiology were all fun for me. I kept changing my major, so it took me 5 years to graduate in Experimental Psychology. The one class that had the greatest impact on included teaching a rat to press a button for his food. I used the skills learned to help me with becoming a successful teacher.

After graduation, I lost contact with the counselor. She knew that I chose to get married and probably assumed that I wouldn't go to graduate school. After I separated from my husband, eleven years had passed since I last saw her. I decided to write and tell her that I had separated form Abani and was in therapy. I also told her that I had started back to school to begin my courses for my master's degree. Since the counselor was retired, the school forwarded the letter to her at home. She responded and sent me a letter in return. I never opened it. I regret that today. I was afraid of what was in the letter. I was afraid that she would be angry at me. I was afraid that I had disappointed her.

My first experience at a gynecologist's office was devastating. At the age of 21, I visited one for the first time. I had pain in my abdomen. He did a routine check and said there were no problems. He then proceeded to finger-fuck me. Stiffening every cell in my body, barely breathing, I didn't respond to his invasion.

I froze and didn't move until he was done.

Seeing no response from me, he gave up. I have no idea if he got his jollies from getting women to climax or if he was preparing to rape me. All I could see was that my feet were in the stirrups and my vagina was open and an easy target. I didn't report him. It would have been my word against his. There was no one else in the room.

It wasn't until I was seventy years old and speaking with my primary physician that I finally mentioned what happened to me at my first appointment with the gynecologist. I never told anyone, not even Charlotte my therapist, who helped me overcome my childhood abuse.

That wasn't my only negative experience in college. One evening a friend of mine and I decided to go to a Frat party. As we walked through the door, I was groped by a man standing at the entrance. It was as if it was my ticket to get into the party. I told my friend I was leaving. I turned around, left, never to return to another frat party.

Even though I had a couple of boyfriends in high school and in college, I never had sex with them, and the relationships never lasted very long. Often, I would drive to another University and listen to chamber music. As I was leaving the concert, a man yelled. I guess I didn't hear him at first. He was telling me to stop, he wanted to say hello. I ran away all the way across the parking lot to my car. To say the least, I had trouble trusting men. After the gynecologist experience, trusting male doctors would be challenging all my life.

In college, I participated in anti-war protests and often went to hootenannies. Fliers were put up around the campus, and I always made a point to go. Hootenannies were a songfest. Strangers usually would sit around a living room, someone would hand out papers with words to songs and the person playing the guitar would start playing. We sang both folk songs and anti-war songs. I enjoyed this. I didn't have to be friends with anyone, I didn't have to say much, and I didn't have to connect with any young men. Once a young man sitting next to me told me that I had a very strong voice. Embarrassed, I mumbled thank you and ignored him the rest of the evening.

During my college junior and senior years, I hung out in with a small group of girlfriends. We went to concerts and lectures together. One of the girls had a 1949 maroon Hudson, we called it *the beast*. It was big enough for all of us to fit into when we went places. However, it was only good for short hops. After all, it was almost twenty years old and not very reliable.

We decided to go to Palm Springs for spring break, but we needed a car that was dependable. We piled into my '63 yellow and brown Chevy and headed out for a glorious week. In Palm Springs, at night we would drive down the main thoroughfare, scream and holler out the window at the young men just like everyone else. We did go to some parties but didn't participate in the drinking and drugs. We met some young men, but we were really interested in doing girl things and didn't go there to hook up with someone. It was just what I needed.

Marriage

I met Abani on a blind date set up by an acquaintance in one of my college classes who was married to a man from Pakistan. After I met Abani, we spent all our time with people from India or Pakistan. I no longer hung out with my college friends. We dated for several months before he asked me to marry him. He treated me well at the beginning of the relationship, but as time passed, he became possessive and controlling. I was a possession.

One day we went out to a lake for a picnic. He was driving his small British sports car and ran into a very large rock after turning into the parking lot. He yelled at me because I didn't tell him that there was a large rock near the front right tire. I never saw the rock; I wasn't paying any attention to where he was driving. I thought that was his responsibility, but apparently, it was all my fault.

Probably the most egregious red flag was the systemic removal of my circle of friends. Even though we got married right after I graduated from college, I no longer communicated with or had contact with my college friends.

At one point a couple of months before graduation and our marriage, I threw my engagement ring at him; I was done. I don't even remember the argument. However, "I'm sorry, please take me back, I will never do it again," became the mantra that I repeatedly heard from then on.

Toward the end of my last quarter of college, I was walking down some steep stairs to the lower parking lot, to reach my car. I stepped wrong, fell and twisted my ankle. It was considered a bad sprain, so the student health center put me on crutches and wrapped my ankle. I was on crutches for quite a while.

Since my counselor was on leave, I made an appointment to see the head psychologist of the university center. As I entered the room where he was, the first question out of his mouth was "You come in here all crippled. What is it you are trying to stop yourself from doing?"

Confrontational psychology is not what I needed at the time. I needed to be heard, I needed to verbalize what was bothering me. Isn't this the same thing that happened to me when I was thirteen and needed to speak with someone when I went to the nurse's office? I turned around and left.

One week before the wedding we visited the minister who was going to marry us. Mr. Bennett gave both Abani and me a personality test. Abani's test came back with two dome-shaped curves at either end of the horizontal scale. As politely as possible, Mr. Cleveland suggested that living with an individual with this profile would be very difficult. He was trying to tell me not to marry him while keeping his ethical requirements intact. I had no courage to stop the wedding.

I thought about what he said, but we were having a large wedding in a few days. We had visitors from India who came specifically for the wedding. I didn't have the guts to not go through with the wedding. Today, my children tell me that they wouldn't be who they are if I had not married Abani.

I am good at rationalizing. I told myself that since English is his second language, that is why he did poorly on the personality test. What a ridiculous thought! Abani had spoken English as well as the native language of his country since he was a child. I married a man who was manipulative, controlling and verbally abusive.

Throughout the first summer of the marriage, I worked in a local department store as a cashier. I had been accepted at a local university in the fall to begin a Master's program leading to a Ph.D. I had told Abani many times before our wedding that I had planned to enter graduate school and get my master's in child psychology. I intended to complete my Ph.D. He never said anything for or against that idea before we wed.

Three weeks after we were married, he told me that he didn't want me to have a Ph.D. because he had no intention upon furthering his own education. He wanted me to go to work, not to school. I watched as he cheated his way to his bachelor's degree by copying someone else's senior project and said nothing.

Not wanting to get into another fight, I did my student teaching while continuing to work. I persuaded myself that I could be self-actualized without my Ph.D. My efforts to please him increased, thinking that I was the problem. I wore saris, let my hair grow and wore long skirts.

We argued almost every night. I couldn't do anything right. Why weren't the cupboards cleaned out? The dinner was terrible; don't I know how to cook? The lunch I packed for him didn't have this or that in it. Everything that came out of his mouth took me by surprise. I would fix one thing that he complained about, and he immediately found something else. I couldn't believe how I could fail so miserably. The number of things that I did wrong was overwhelming. I couldn't do anything right!

I know that the workers in the store where I went to work every morning saw my puffy eyes. No one said anything. I passed it off as newlywed problems. I had no one to talk with. I was very much alone.

I did my student teaching and applied for a teaching position. My ability to communicate with children, my background in psychology, and an inborn natural ability to work with children helped me become very successful. I enjoyed what I was doing. Besides, children were safe.

As Abani aged, he gradually became more and more conservative in his attitudes and expected Indian behavior from me. More importantly, his demand for control and his abusiveness increased with each day. Throughout the entire eleven years, we were married, we argued and fought. He tried only once to hit me, but I hit back. He then went to verbal abuse when I couldn't do anything in return. In the car, he would grab my hand and put either my thumb or finger in his mouth and then bite down as hard as he could. I couldn't pull my hand away. Unable to move, unable to do anything to him for fear of wrecking the car, I would just sit there screaming. He did this for years even after we had children and they were sitting in the back seat of the car.

The more I tried to please him, the more I did things wrong (in his eyes). It seemed as if I was walking on eggshells, any misstep and I would break an egg, and he would be angry. His anger seemed to come from nowhere unexpectedly and most often surprise me. He often criticized that I laughed too loud in public, or that dinner was too hot, the next night it was too cold, or the house was a mess.

When I was barraged by how much I had failed at everything and had enough, I would try and leave the room. Abani would grab my arm, stand in the way, close the door and stand in front of it to keep me from getting away from him. He forced me to listen to his tirade.

He controlled the money. Therefore he controlled what I bought for myself, clothes, makeup, etc. I began to look very haggard, old and was very depressed. Once at Yosemite, I wanted to buy a Tee shirt that had a tiger on it. He told me that in no way could I buy the shirt and wear it, I was certainly no tiger!

He would always go with me when buying clothes. He even chose my clothes. Older women during that time would wear knit suits. He purchased three of them for me. The sales lady came up to me and whispered that the clothes were for much older women. I came home with three matronly knit suits and wore them.

When we visited India, I realized that there was no way I could stay and make the marriage work. I had had enough. Upon returning to the US, I planned to file for divorce but became pregnant within a few days of returning home. I blame it on jet lag. I decided to stay and attempt to make the marriage work. Maybe I could change. I tried everything that I knew to make things better, but it never seemed to make any difference. And now I was pregnant.

When my daughter was two and a half, I became pregnant with my son. A couple of months later, I tried to leave out the front door with my daughter in my arms. Abani grabbed my arm and pulled me back, making me lose my grip on my daughter. Fortunately, I was able to hold onto her, and I didn't drop her. He positioned himself in front of the door and stopped me. Again, there was the mantra, "I will stop. I will change. Don't go. I will change."

Cries of Freedom

I had made a mental decision in college that I would do a better job of raising my children than my parents did in raising me. I took courses in child development and P.E.T. (Parent Effectiveness Training). Not only did I learn of a variety of healthful ways to raise children, but I also had an opportunity to practice those techniques at home and in the elementary school classroom. I was always interfacing with at least one child that needed some positive intervention during the day. I found that I accomplished a lot more when I analyzed a situation or found a constructive way to handle it. My skills at working with children increased each day.

Despite my ability to work with children, I exploded one night when my daughter was four, and my son was two. At midnight, my daughter got out of bed and woke me up. She was wheezing. I took her to the dining area where her medication was and started filling the nebulizer. So very tired, sleep deprived and unable to cope with my miserable marriage, I pounded and hammered the oak dining room table with my right arm. I couldn't believe my anger. I couldn't believe my strength. I might have killed my daughter! Terrified of my own anger, I took care of her medication, tucked her into bed and cried all night. (The bruising on my forearm, wrist and elbow, from hammering it on the table, lasted for over a month).

While at school, I called the school psychologist and asked him to suggest a therapist. I was afraid that the next time I would hurt my children. He gave me the name of a group that works with women in crisis. I was able to see a therapist that afternoon.

Cries for Freedom

The silver headed eagle screams for freedom
The Minotaur, keys in hand, laughs.
"What is this selfish bird wanting?
What sort of price will she pay?
Freedom is not for anyone who only pleads for one day."

The eagle bangs her beak on the ribs of her cage.
Blood spurts out.
Yet the evil Minotaur hears no call.
He makes no effort to help the poor bird out.

The week after my first visit with a therapist, I came home ill from teaching school. I called Abani (it was after 4:00 P.M.) and asked if he would come home and watch the children; who were now two and four years old. Forty minutes later, he wasn't home. I called his work again. This time his boss answered and I asked if Abani had left. I explained the situation and his boss said he would send him home.

When Abani entered the house, he said to me, "Don't ever call me to come home from work again to take care of children!" The next day, I called Charlotte and asked her what she thought. Her comment to me was, "How much more are you going to take?"

I had been perching on an emotional cliff for a long time; I finally jumped off and filed for divorce the next day which was Friday. That evening, I called the police, and they escorted Abani out of the house. However, Abani spent the entire week (until my next visit with Charlotte) calling everyone that knew me. He called members of my family, the clergyman who married us, and the principal of the school where I was teaching, asking them to please call me and tell me to take him back. He even saw Charlotte.

At my next visit with Charlotte, she suggested that he and I spend an afternoon together to see if there was anything that could be salvaged from the marriage. I feared that she too was going to make me go back with him. If I had to go back with Abani, I would rather have died. I can honestly say that there was not one good day in the marriage. It was wrong from the beginning, and I knew it. During our engagement we had many fights, two months before the wedding; I broke up with him, broke my ankle, and slept for three days the week before the wedding. I just didn't listen to my body.

Charlotte told me that if I wanted to get back with Abani, I would need to find another therapist because Abani was extremely manipulative and she was easily manipulated. She couldn't work with both of us.

Two weeks after my separation, depression surfaced. I wrote a suicide letter. Even though I was despondent, I went to my next meeting with Charlotte. I showed her my suicide note. After working with me for a short period of time trying to get me to show anger, she told me that either I give her the name of my doctor so I could get some medication or she would put me into the hospital. All I wanted to do was to leave and disappear. After her insistence, I agreed to give her permission to call my doctor. I had to see her every day for a week.

She helped me realize that no one was going to make me go back with him if I didn't want to go back. The next week we started a three-year journey together to help me heal.

Incest

Beauty, its skin unmarred
Is but a crimson letter of olden days.
Whether it be beauty of mind,
Spirit, heart or body,
It quickly turns to black ash
When with malice my child embrace is answered.

My soul hides within the ashes
No one knows I'm here
No one cares
I am safe.

Decades later, smoke from the ashes
Sculpts my soul.
Fear, pain, illness follow.
Mountains, obstacles, roads and bridges interfere.
To become, begin, endure.
I am again.

Incest

In the poem "Incest," I talk about a normal touch between children and adults turning to ash when a child's touch is answered with malice. It is when touch no longer is a healthy touch, but one that is hostile to the developing child, that serious damage occurs. Incest can best be understood with this analogy.

Suppose my father asks me if I wanted a chocolate-dipped vanilla ice cream cone (my favorite ice cream cone as a child). Instead, he gives me vanilla mixed with chopped onions, and dill pickles, because that was his favorite flavor. Then he manipulates, persuades and cajoles me so that I would try it. I wanted to please, and I was a sweet little girl, so I did what I was told to do. Mixed-in with the vanilla/ dill pickle/ onion ice cream is something to make me very ill, causing me to vomit and cripple me with a lifelong illness. This scenario is repeated and repeated. Each time, my father manipulated, cajoled, and persuaded me into eating the ice cream with threats that he wouldn't love me any more or that he would tell my mother, and she, in turn, would be very angry with me. So I ate the ice cream and became ill.

It's all about control.

Where is the Little Girl?

Where is the little girl? I am the little girl. You can tell I was there because my porcelain doll, dressed in a fancy dress with ribbons in her hair, is safely tucked away in the tree roots. The swing is still warm. I was just swinging. Elmer called me away and molested me.

Even though my family was active in the church and Elmer taught Sunday school the entire time he was molesting me, the church knew nothing about it. I kept the family secret to myself. It's difficult to understand how no one knew what kind of man he was. He seemed to fool everyone.

The Tiger of Despair

My heart swelled with pride
I was in love and it felt so fine.
I was young, I was bold
I knew of no tiger nor felt its breath so cold.

When he hugged me I felt alive.
He was so gentle, so loving, mine.
I played horsy sitting on his foot, I'd go flying
I had no fear.
But the Tiger grew with each passing year.

At forty-one he was the apple of my eye.
I trusted, I did what I was told
I was only five.
I did not understand,
The tiger of despair was at hand.

At ten, the days grew long
I lost all feeling, I was gone.
Pushed off the bed, naked and scared
I crawled to my room severed!

The unspoken words shouted!
The tension mounted
Boy-style haircut, jeans and tees,
My mother was pleased.

I was destroyed.
The tiger of despair had won.

Barbara Weber   51

Like all little girls, by the age of three, I was in love with my Daddy. At that time, I remember him as an extremely busy man, teaching at the University, and working during the summer to support a large family. My most fond memory is standing next to him in church while we were singing a hymn. I couldn't read, didn't know the words, and had to stand on the pew to see, but I sang with great enthusiasm. I felt proud. Often after dinner, I would sit on his foot when he had his legs crossed, he would kick his foot into the air and give me a ride.

I wrote the poem "The Tiger of Despair" to describe what happened to me. After my brother caught Elmer and me on the bed, the abuse stopped. Marie cut my hair after I showed her the quarter when I was seven. She later told me that she thought the abuse had stopped at that time. When seven, she made no mistake. She not only cut my hair short but dressed me in my brother's old clothes. At one point she laughed when some new friends couldn't tell whether or not I was a girl or a boy. I guess this was her way of making me less attractive and therefore protected from further abuse.

To this day I am unable to picture myself between the ages of five, the beginning of my molestation, and ten or eleven, my age when the molestation stopped. I have some pictures of me taken during that time period. When I look at them, I don't recognize them as me.

During therapy I described my body as such:

I picture a body, legs, arms, and trunk. They are shaped just like ceramic plumbing pipe, only made of cardboard, empty inside. Replacing my head is a devil head with distorted eyes, nose, and mouth. It is black and red and so ugly that it is difficult to keep its image in my head. Hinges and string hold the body together. Unable to move on its own, the body is an object to be moved at the will of anyone. I am not there. I have taken me out of the body and do not feel a thing.

As I continued through therapy, I became aware that this viewpoint of my body continued during sex. I could be manipulated, moved however my partner wished. (I labeled this behavior the plastic doll syndrome). Once I began to change my attitude about myself, I attracted a different kind of man, and the plastic doll syndrome disappeared. Sometime during therapy, I replaced the hollow tubes with substance. The submissive thin string at the core of my being was changed to a steel rod.

I Cry a Tear, I Make a Frown

A baby is born look and see.
A baby girl who wants to be free.
I cry a tear, I make a frown
She has made her first sound.

Oh, little girl, what is wrong?
A swat, a yardstick, a fly swatter now?
It will only hurt a little while.
I cry a tear, I make a frown
A toddler tries to make a sound.

At three she hides her talent
For just a little while.
It's better now, less spanking, more love
I cry a tear, I make a frown
Creativity has drowned.

Deception at five proves to be too much
She's different, she understands, she knows
To be loved and accepted, the entire brain needs to be closed.
I cry a tear, I make a frown
Someone inside is painted brown.

Thirteen proves to be too much, more alterations are needed.
Blinders, ear muffs, keep out the world.
A game keeps in the love.
I cry a tear, I make a frown,
Intelligence went underground.

Twenty-one years later
The self-cries out for freedom.
The little girl cries,
"Unleash my shackles, untie my bonds!
I want to be free!"

I cry a tear, a frown I do not make
For this day of freedom, I can hardly wait.

I Cry a Tear I Make a Frown

I used brick and mortar helmet as an impenetrable defense to protect myself from harm. As a child, I was unable to think, play or "be" without criticism. I invented ways in which to cope. The poem "I Cry a Tear, I Make a Frown," describes the methods I used to maintain control — to cope. I felt these controls help me to keep me sane.

Charlotte had me to draw a picture of my poem and then write what would happen without my defenses. Here is the picture of my brick house covering me.

I Cry a Tear, I Make a Frown

Below is the explanation for this painting that I wrote in my journal after I finished painting this picture.

I took my creativity and my problem-solving ability and enclosed them. The cement covering was impenetrable. The red space at the bottom of the painting illustrated hot lava. The lava was slowly eating me away.

Insanity is the out of control explosion of ideas and feelings. Brown dirty stagnated goo squirting out all over, exploding with red and yellow in all directions. Heavy feelings detonate into smaller particles. There is no form, no container, goo goes in all directions forming no basic shape except to finally disappear. The explosion goes from inside out, and once all parts are disassembled and disseminated, they go into outer space and are never formed again together as anything. On to eternity; it is the end of the contained self.

To keep this from happening, I imagined an armored plate-like metal helmet around my head. This protected me from lightning. Lightning signifies electricity which is an extremely strong, loud, cracking, frightening force exemplifying a lack of control. Power comes from the outside force. I can't control the direction. It is out of my control.

If the lightning is allowed to enter, it is hot and sharp. It burns as it enters. It can enter anywhere the eyes, the heart, the stomach, the mind. As it enters it leaves a burned path of destruction hurting forever. I remember the sharp pain of the hot spike. It comes from outward and enters and burns. It represents the cutting words that sizzle as a branding iron would when it is touched on the hide of a steer. The looks of disgust, hatred, misunderstanding. The feelings, oh my the feelings. How awful. What did I do wrong?

The armor plate deflects the lightning. As long as it remains, no heat can get through and burn. No sharp point can cut sting and puncture its soft tissue. The shield is permanent and gives me security. I don't really want it off. Possibly underneath is deteriorated. I see it as dry and shriveled.

On the forehead of the picture of my head is a red wall which symbolizes hot molten magma. This magma sloshes around and is ready to pour out in the event of an explosion. It too will destroy everything in its path. The wall keeps it in. If the wall is broken down or destroyed the hot magma would then became lava and pour out and destroy everything in its path. The wall keeps it contained.

My crazy picture was the first picture that I painted. I felt strongly that I was losing my mind. The round object in the center represented me. I was covered in cement unable to think or feel. The lightning on the left expressed the fact that I felt like I had to dodge the lightning, it was constantly hitting me. The explosion on the right illustrates my inability to feel in control. At any moment I was going to explode. The pyramid on the right-hand side of my mind (right hand as you look at it) has a symbol of me. Notice at this point there is nothing there but a symbol. This symbol had no depth, no meaning other than that of a soul which illustrated my shallow existence. The right side of the mind (the left side of the painting) illustrated my intelligence. I was not using my intelligence. It was completely encased in cement a non-moving static substance.

The yellow triangle represents me; plain surrounded by nothingness, dull, lifeless, blah and uninteresting. There is no sunlight on this mind. There is no coolness of healing. Only heat of war, conflict, hell. For sanity to occur, I had to integrate. Total self. It was the ability to bring to mind what I wish, no faking, no games; its beauty at its finest hour. Yellow, blue, green intermingle, leaving a hue of radiance unequaled in my creativity on the right side and my high intellectual ability on the left side.

I envisioned high rises, steam shovels and various shapes on the left side of the mind. These illustrated a working city. Before thinking about it, the steam shovels were still, the high rises empty and the various shapes were static shapes. I believe my symbolism here stands for my ability to function intellectually in the world. Shapes represented mathematical ability, machines represented problem-solving ability and the high rises represented allowing me to reach to the sky and take chances with my abilities. I'm not sure why I put the frog in the picture, but maybe I felt very much alone and stuck on a rock surrounded by water unable to move off of the rock. I used a frog in the picture so the ability to move from the rock was there, I just hadn't moved yet

As the work continued and I began to be comfortable with who I was, I began to think of what was on my mind. I thought of my mind in two halves.

•   •   •   •   •

I have left this explanation intact. I don't think I could do a better job in describing how I felt.

Feeling like I was being attacked by everyone, I protected myself by using a strong fortress type helmet. I used a wolf as the guardian of that fortress. The symbolism surfaced many times during therapy. I was very much afraid of facing the "pack of wolves" harbored within me.

Two Halves of my Brain

Two halves in my brain.
Two cities each unique.
Each having a section as its own place.
One full of colors, animals and shapes
The other more open,
Using silver, black, white and gray
To make all necessary objects for each day.

One side is warm, the other cool.
One has beauty the other functional.
They are separated by a barrier,
Yet somehow seem to work together.

On the cool side, waiting for instructions,
A tall silver erector steam shovel sits.
With a large building all shiny and bright
Waiting for someone to enter
And turn on the lights.
Metallic furniture resides,
Modern, yet with memories of childhood.
All of these waiting for someone to discover and find.

The warm side screams with delight
Colors of music, love and fun alight,
Here are streets with houses, animals
Shapes and feelings.
This side by far is the most appealing.

Both sides wait to be explored
Both sides wait with patience.
No one comes.

Barbara Weber   57

Charlotte asked me how I could find out what exists under the cement covering of my brain. I suggested using a helicopter to see the streets. That night, I wrote "High in my Helicopter."

High in My Helicopter

High in my helicopter, I see a beautiful place
With many colorful streets etched on its face.
Colors of friendship, happiness and love
Beckon me to come down from above,
Red, yellow, lavender and green closely mimic my every dream.

Purple houses illuminate against a lavender sky.
Each one tells a different story, not one tells a lie.
The house I like best sits on the corner
A little girl sits on the stoop,
Elbows on knees, hands under chin,
She's dreaming of love, fellowship and kin.

The loudest street calls with orange, yellow and red. come bounce, come
slide, come play again.
The huge geometric shapes, some standing, some on their sides,
Leave lots of room to run and hide.

By far the most beautiful is the green music place.
It's filled with sweet melodies, swans, butterflies and lace.
The street is for relaxing, meditating and spirit healing and by far the most
sensually appealing.

More beauty exists in my sacred place
More avenues each different and unique.
I need only to land and spend a day,
Just feeling, touching and basking in its radiant rays.

Barbara Weber   59

On the left side of my brain, I envisioned high rises, steam shovels, and various shapes. To me these illustrated a working city. The steam shovels were still, high rises empty and the various shapes were static shapes. Shapes represented mathematical ability, machines represented problem-solving ability, and the high rises represented me reaching to the sky taking chances.

When I finished writing the poem "Two Halves of my Brain" and painting a picture depicting the poem, I ended up with a horrible headache. One right on top of my eyebrows and around my eyes. I went to bed and dreamed that I was mad at my ex-husband concerning money. I chased him, and he ran (this was unusual). Usually, I am the one that was being chased. He ran to the street, and I stomped on his stomach. I woke up with a headache thinking about the picture of my mind.

Charlotte and I discussed what it might take to get the machinery started. I was fearful that removing the protective covering on my head might reveal that there was nothing underneath or that I was insane, unable to function and/or stupid.

I decided that returning to school to complete my master's degree would be a way to get the machinery moving. Now it seems so simple. I did go back to school, and within ten months of beginning therapy, I achieved my Master's Degree in Special Education "Gifted." However, it really wasn't that easy. I kept putting obstacles in my way. For instance, on my way to the school to register, I made a wrong turn, and I kept forgetting necessary items to complete my registration.

The Right Side of My Brain

I taught myself to play the piano when I was very young. At the University school, all students in the fourth grade were required to take up an instrument. I learned to play the clarinet. So I played both instruments. After my divorce, I purchased a piano and played it every day. It calmed me down. I also purchased a large wooden flute. I learned to play it as well.

I realized that hiking, camping or walking in the outdoors centered me. To me, there was nothing better but to get up early in the morning and take a walk whether it be in the desert, the mountains with snow or on the seashore.

The painting represented my vision of my creative side. Flowers took on a vibrant color, and the sky was a beautiful blue. Music could be heard and beat a rhythm that matched my own heartbeat.

Left Side of the Brain

This is the first picture that I painted of the left side of my brain. After a few weeks, I painted the picture with the frog and removed the geese. This was painted on heavy paper using acrylics. It was never framed and has been floating around in my closet. The extra painting smudges on the left are from subsequent paintings. I have thought about going over the smudges to clean them up. The painting is old, and I am beyond the emotional challenges that I initially painted. I have opted to leave the smudges.

Barbara Weber 63

This is the second picture that I painted. It is oil on canvas. Many of my paintings include geometric shapes and a symbol of life such as flowers or animals. I'm not sure why I put the frog in this picture, but maybe I felt very much alone and stuck on a rock. I was surrounded by water and unable to move. However, frogs jump, and maybe I just hadn't moved yet.

Within a year and a half, I completed my Master's Degree. The frog jumped off the rock.

One in Seven

Being different has never been a solace or comfort for me. I have always felt somewhat isolated and not able to fit in. It wasn't until I was much older that I realized my differences were strengths. There were many times in school where I would get ahead of the teacher (especially in math) and must "wait for the class" to catch up. Even picking up a game called "Instant Insanity" (a general Christmas present to the family) and solving it within seconds, made me feel like an oddball. No one wanted to figure out how to solve it after I did. I spoiled the game for everyone.

When three, I would watch my mother write a letter. (She would write to her mother regularly). On my own, I would take a piece of paper and write what I saw her write. My older brother would come in and cruelly tell me that I don't know what I am writing; I don't know how to spell either. That stopped me from ever copying her writing again.

This brother teased me viciously all the time. When visiting me in the past year, he mentioned how he teased me. He said that at one point I threw a pipe and it hit him in the face. My response was "good." My mother should have stopped him, but she never did. The teasing was constant and brutal.

My mother, Marie, liked to play cards. I used to watch her play Canasta with my brother and sister. At the age of four, I asked to play. I needed help melding, but I won. After that, no one wanted to play with me. The Canasta games stopped. I blamed myself for that. I have always thought I was dumb and there was something wrong with me.

I drew this picture and then dyed silk to make a painting to represent how I feel. I am different! In the picture, the different colored bird represents me. The shapes, bold colors, and seemingly replicated pattern with a slight misalignment reflect where I am in the world. I don't express to the outside world my uniqueness or differences. I am still hiding. I have hidden from the limelight all

Barbara Weber   65

of my life. I have never wanted to be noticed. After all, if I am noticed, then I might be molested again.

As I grew older. I did take some risks. In Anchorage, I would participate in what is called First Friday. This is where I would show my paintings at a coffee shop. The public would walk around downtown and look at the artists' shows. I sold several paintings the short time I participated. I even had one stolen from the front of a gallery.

All of my paintings are signed BJ Ellis. I don't like my maiden name, and I don't like my first married name. BJ stands for my first and middle names, and Ellis is a name I made up. I liked the sound of it, BJ Ellis!

My Quiet Place

My Quiet Place (1997)

During therapy there were times when I had to confront difficult and upsetting issues. My therapist would ask me to imagine a quiet place where I could go and feel safe. There was a stream, with trees and rocks. I would often sit under the tree or on a rock and watch the wildlife as they wandered nearby. The sun was warm, the sky blue and flowers aromatic. When sitting on a rock near the stream, I would put my feet in the cool water and let the water rush over my toes. The little waterfall represented my old self going downstream and a new one emerging from the water upstream.

Barbara Weber   67

My Guide

My Guide (2005)

In therapy sessions, I often came to a point where I couldn't go any further. I called these places psychological walls, mountains or a fork in the road. I was unsure of which path to take, so my therapist asked me to ask my guide. He would always show me which path to take or what I needed to do to go around the obstacle or climb the wall. He was never wrong.

I didn't paint this picture of my guide until years later. I find I still need him. He is cloaked in a brown hooded coat, has a beard, a long cane and is very wise. He has guided me on a long journey across rivers of great difficulty. The sun is shining on him as he directs me on my path. I have him hanging above my desk in my office where he can continue to guide me every day.

Barbara Weber 69

Metaphorical Houses

When in session with Charlotte, she always listened and was very good at directing me toward insight or solution to a problem. Almost every visit, I would mention a dream, a poem or a painting. Writing poems was easy. I'd sit in bed at night, and the poems would almost write themselves. They are not sophisticated and would never be anything on their own, but they served a purpose for me.

My dreams on the other hand centered on certain themes, houses, monsters, animals (wolves), deformed or hurt babies, pain/injury, entrapment, sinister people, bait and switch and violation of my peace and security.

Of my theme dreams, my house dreams were probably the most predominant. I dreamt about many different kinds of houses in a variety of geographical locations. Each house represented a distinct emotion, peace, stress, looking for something, hostility, cold, distant, distress, indecisiveness, confusion, pain, and a house that needs work. The same houses would reoccur at various times. The events were usually different, but the emotion usually remained the same. When I stopped dreaming about a house, I assume I resolved some sort of issue. Here are a couple of examples of my houses and dreams.

Some houses were two story, some ranch and none looked like any house I ever lived in or experienced. Most had an outside and an inside, but some were only seen from a specific angle. Many fit within a neighborhood with specific characteristics and some did not have a normal room plan.

For example, one apartment located in a concrete building was situated near the ocean. Sometimes I would be on the patio, at other times I would be inside. A cold and distant couple lived there. They had a very small kitchen and only one other room. To me, this apartment represented cold and distant emotions.

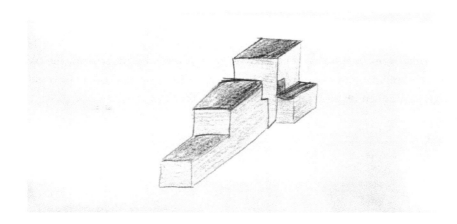

Other ocean dreams sometimes included this apartment house but the tide was always coming in and water flooded over me. Most often, the water pulled me offshore and I was unable to get back. In a sense, I was drowning with the waves crashing over me. I was in a hopeless situation.

This dream took place in other locations, the sandy ocean beach, at the end of a highway, but always, I was overwhelmed with the rushing water. I never got away, I always woke up first.

Eleven years after I completed therapy, the dream was finally resolved. I dreamt that I was walking along a cement walkway next to a concrete wall. The walkway was down toward the ocean from the cement apartment building. The other side of the walkway was also a high cement wall.

As I walked down a steep walkway, the enclosure morphed into a pit. I was at the bottom of the pit. Water was released and quickly filled the pit like a pool. Soon to be overcome with rushing water (I couldn't find a way out, and I couldn't find the valve to turn the water off), I realized that I was a good swimmer and if I hung on to the sides I would float to the top. I floated to the top and walked away. I never had that dream again

Other house scenarios occurred in Hollywood. I dreamt about the same street of houses many times. One specific time, I was looking for a dress for my daughter, but the house had spices, candles, and homemade craft items. We left three of my daughter's dolls in the house for an old woman to repair them. When we returned, she had died. No one could get anything until her will was read. I was very upset. "Who would want to take a five-year-old child's dolls? Who would be so mean to do that?" I thought in my dream.

Two other houses were on the same block but down the street from the old lady who had my daughter's dolls. One house was white, situated on a steep hill. It could only be seen by looking through a tree in the front yard.

The other house was small and green. It had leaves all around it. There was no tree. I retrieved the dolls from the greenhouse.

A ranch house situated in an urban west coast setting represented distress. Two trees stood in front. It was white stucco and had a double entryway with green grass in front. The house was always seen from a left angle instead of straight on. I realize I drew the side of the house as brown, but in my dream, they were white.

Usually, my dreams about the following floor plan house took place inside of it. It was back east somewhere, huge with a variety of rooms. It consisted of many different levels with small rooms and needed a lot of repairs. My two children and my mother moved in with me. It had a big backyard with numerous neighbors.

Symbolic Dreams

In addition to dreams involving houses, I had nightmares with monsters. I was always running from them. Often I dreamt about the same monster. This was a terrifying nightmare because no matter what I did, I couldn't get away from him. One time, the monster caught up with me, I stopped, turned and found out that the monster was not scary but very friendly and nice. It turned out that this monster was me.

One night, I was dreaming about walking next to a pasture of grazing sheep, and a wolf attacked me. He punctured and clawed both of my legs. The following week, when I saw Charlotte, I could still feel and "see" the holes in my leg. We worked using imagery on healing those wounds. The wounds were healed, but the scars remain.

Dolls or babies were always present. In one specific dream, I saw a young girl put a baby in the gutter. I ran and picked it up. It had no head, and the body was a burned shell. After putting the baby in a blanket, I put a chicken heart into the body and massaged the heart. It felt good to hold this baby. I liked the warmth. After a time, I looked down, and the baby was alive and kicking.

Other dreams involved meeting people that seem to be normal but had a wickedness about them. For instance, at a pond, I met seven monks. They spoke Turkish. Along came someone from Greece and they had an argument. I was fascinated by the monks, so I followed them to a secret underwater passageway to their city-like compound (where they lived). I was able to see the inner workings of the compound.

Their compound had a castle with various condos built on hills. All were connected by passageways. The people working for the monks were actually slaves and used to farm their crops. They were also mistreated and forced to do heavy labor. On the outside, these monks seemed like honest religious people. Yet they were not.

The FBI had found the little city and put it under siege. As the monks left, many cars broke down. The Levee protecting the city broke, and the compound flooded. Government personnel drained the compound and began excavating to find out about monks' way of life.

Bait and switch is a common theme probably reflecting how I was manipulated into passiveness when abused. I bought tickets or went somewhere expecting normal events to occur but found that I was deceived. For instance, I dreamt that I had purchased a ticket on United Airlines. As I entered the airport, I looked for the gate. The building was very fancy and modern, but I couldn't find the gate. I eventually found it on the other side of the airport. It required walking along a sidewalk next to a lake or seashore. Of course, there was a small wall, and I walked on the small wall, the way children often do. However, the airlines had been switched, and instead of United Airlines, I was flying on *Swampers* Express. I became very angry that United would mislead the public and sell tickets on a small old turbojet. I went back to United to change the tickets to a regular airline and woke up.

Many other dreams involved a hostage or trapped situation. For instance, I was held hostage with a group of other people my age. I believe I was young. Finally, able to escape, a horde of army ants came after me. Even, jumping in water didn't drown the ants, they continued to get under my clothes and bite me. I finally climbed a hill, became stuck under some impossible underbrush, managed to wiggle out and find a bus with medical help. After four days I entered a big city hospital. I didn't speak, just stared and answered questions without uttering a sound.

Consequently, I was put into a ward for the mentally disturbed and would lay on the bed like a vegetable. I eventually decided to get up and move to another room when my friends visited me. We had a happy reunion even though I couldn't talk.

To this day, when I feel trapped and feel that circumstances have made it impossible for me to escape, I become suicidal.

Perseverance

Perseverance

I struggled for almost three and a half years in therapy. The "Tired Old Woman" was written during a time when I became exhausted and discouraged. I painted *Perseverance* because I felt it visually depicted my struggle. I felt like I was balancing glass objects on the point of glass pyramids in order to find a way to a "normal" life.

Barbara Weber   77

A Tired Old Woman

As I sit by the window.
My heart cries out in anguish.
To love and be loved in this world
Is truly a gift.
The one most important reason for living

A good life is for only a few.
The rest must struggle in torment.
All for what purpose?
Mine has been shattered in the wind.

What is life but a torment of unattainable wishes and hopes
The insurmountable mountains that must be surpassed?
Only to find more, on to infinity.
For as I reach closer to walking on the path toward a goal
The obstacles are overwhelming.

It would be wonderful to live a life
Enriched and to its fullest.
I won't be so lucky, for my meaningless worthless life to end,
Would bring such great satisfaction.
There is nothing worse than to live a
Loveless, purposeless and senseless life.

A Mother's Protection

Worried about my children and knowing the cycle abuse continues from one generation to the next unless specific action is taken, I was determined to stop the cycle of abuse. I thought that since I had divorced my husband and I was working on me, I had put an end to it. I was wrong.

Soon after my ex-husband and I divorced, he would hold my son down so he couldn't move and bite him all over his body. When the bite marks were bad enough to last many hours, I saw them when Abani dropped him home after a visit. As soon as I saw the marks, I took him to the hospital to document and record the bites.

They notified the District Attorney, and he informed me that since my son's skin was not broken, he wasn't hurt bad enough to prosecute the case. He suggested that I obtain a civil suit that would generate a court order to get my ex-husband to stop. When an older more powerful individual holds a child forcibly against his will and then bites the child hard enough to make bite marks all over his body that last for several hours, that is abuse! The District Attorney was concerned about cultural issues interfering with a guilty verdict. The biting continued about one year from its onset to the time that a court order ended it.

Sexual, physical or psychological abuse contains an element of power. Just as I was powerless to stop my father from violating me, my son was powerless to stop his father from biting him. How strong can a three-year-old little boy be? Certainly not strong enough to be able to move away from physically being pinned down.

I spent many months working with my son to help him get over this trauma. We fed the monster that came after him at night. He had many nightmares and had a tremendous amount of anger. At this time, I was dating a man named George. He was working toward in license as a Marriage and Family Counselor. He roughed-housed with my son play-act like he was beating and slashing George with a knife. We could see the anger in my son's eyes. I believe that it was George who helped my son overcome the trauma.

He also saw a child psychologist, and I assume that he has not suffered any lasting ill effects from the biting. He doesn't remember any of it. I left my ex-husband so I could protect my children. I was eventually able to protect my son, but it took a civil lawsuit to get him to stop. Not wishing to pay lawyer fees that I couldn't afford for the rest of my life, I did not go back to court to pursue my ex-husband and his financial obligations. To this day, he has paid a negligible amount of money for the care of his children.

Below is a picture that I painted. Notice the very dark background. The child in the woman's lap looks like my son. The woman's jaw is strong, and her profile resembles mine. Consciously I did not plan for these individuals to resemble anyone in particular. I theorize that subconsciously I was comforting him.

The oversized hand illustrates the care and protection that I was giving my son.

Protection (1983)

Barbara Weber   81

Fear

I have fear
Deeply embedded
Here at the center of my heart.
It's cold and light
Afraid to sit still,
For if it lands
It may never start again.

I have fear
I'm moving too fast
Slow down it calls to me
Slow down:
You'll trip, you'll fall
Be careful!
Can't you hear my call?

Heed
Please heed
I beg of you.
It calls again and again
If I ignore it
I may fall
If I listen I may never start at all.

Integration

Integration (1982)

Barbara Weber   83

One day while meditating, I had the image of this painting. When trying to paint what I had visualized, I found it difficult to match the brightness of the images. No paint existed as bright as I had seen in my mind. However, I managed to paint some semblance of what I had envisioned.

"Integration" illustrates the fact that I was able to integrate all of the various aspects of my personality into one. In the picture, the V symbol represents man (as seen on military uniforms) and the upside-down V represents woman. We have both male and female characteristics in our personalities. I'm not sure of the psychological meaning of this painting. I see it as a balance or an intertwining of the male and female within us.

Outer space represents mystic power. The space is not empty but full of clouds and objects. Maybe this represents my inner mind, and I was beginning to get my emotional power and both my female and male counterparts balance.

To Paint A Symphony

I want to paint a symphony
A very difficult one indeed!
I think I know the theme.
I want to sketch the overture capturing every line.
I want to sketch great detail.
Yet, I am afraid and sketch nothing.

How do I begin, what colors do I use?
Each symphony is so different
Do I begin anew?
Is there no framework, no single method
Proclaiming the universal order of man?

Barbara Weber 85

My Mother Cried

My mother cried
The day the truth came near.
The tears, the shaking body,
All showed great fear.
For I the monster,
Gnashing teeth, and blinking eyes,
Have brought forth memories best left behind.

She denied it at first, then
As she thought, she remembered
Could she have been a silent witness?
Foul air grasped at our throats, suffocating and choking, I couldn't breathe.
Death and destruction were close.

Groping, crying, she tried to explain.
What could she do?
Six children, no skills
We surely would have starved.

I quickly changed the subject
For fear of ruining our day.
It was too heavy.
How high the price of human suffering?
Time heals all.

History is history.
I pulled the truth away.
It was too close,
I let the sun shine again
And my mother cried no more.

During therapy, my path to health was often blocked by insurmountable walls, very high mountains, and many obstacles. One of the obstacles I had to conquer was to confront my parents about what happened to me.

My mother and I were discussing my divorce. I then brought the subject up about my abuse. I asked her why she didn't do anything about it. She said she thought it had stopped. I then asked her why she remained in such an abusive marriage. Why didn't she divorce and protect me? She became very upset and said that in the 1950s, she had six children and no skills. She felt there was nothing she could do. She was powerless and afraid she couldn't support the children on her own.

She told me that she had no idea the abuse lasted as long as it did. She thought it was only one incident. It was at this time that she apologized for the way she treated me as a toddler. Health professionals express that we all have the capability for physically abusing children. The difference between an individual that takes their anger out on a child (a child abuser) and an individual that is not a child abuser is that the adult asks for help. A person who asks others for help in taking care of a sick or crying child when they can't take anymore does not lash out at the child. My mother needed help many times, and she did not ask for it. She needed help when I was a young child, and she needed someone to help me when I was five. She didn't want anyone to know that we were not the "Perfect Leave it to Beaver Family."

I wrote the poem "My Mother Cried" after she left that day. I was optimistic then. I thought that time would heal everything. That is not the case. Time may make traumatic memories fade, but they never go away!

Several years later, I was leaving the area. I was forty-nine and Marie wanted to go out to lunch before I left. She wanted to know exactly what Elmer had done to me; she insisted. I told her he essentially had sex with me. The only thing he did not do was penetrate me. He "came" on me (my child's perception was that he peed on me). He also performed a lot of oral sex and tried to force me to give him blowjobs. I remember one time refusing. I don't have any idea if he eventually succeeded to persuade me.

While at lunch, Marie opened up and told me that after we moved from my birthplace to the Midwest (when I was two years old), when Elmer took the university job. She told me that she had received a note from a neighbor. In the note, the neighbor said that Elmer had molested her granddaughter. This was difficult for her to say.

My thoughts at the time were "Had she done something, he wouldn't have molested me. She could have divorced him or kicked him out of the house. I asked her why she didn't divorce him." Her answer was that she had six children and no skills. There was no job that she had any training for, and she wouldn't be able to support us.

When she found out that he was molesting me and had the huge argument, she thought the abuse had stopped. I reminded her that it continued until I was at least ten until my older brother found us on the bed in the master bedroom. Both Elmer and I were on the bed naked. I was ten or eleven. That is when it stopped. She didn't remember that.

Two weeks later, I had moved out of the area, and Marie had a stroke. She recovered from that first stroke, but a few months later she had another one. The doctors wanted to leave the IV in her and let her sleep to her death, but my older sister insisted that they feed her through a feeding tube to give her a chance to recover. She never did and was stuck in a bed unable to feed herself, speak or to walk. She finally died six months later at the age of 87.

Years before I took my mother out to lunch and she insisted I tell her what happened, she had a chance to find out what Elmer had done to me. At that point in time, she refused to talk with me.

Charlotte had asked me to confront my parents. I mailed my mother Susan Forward's book about sexual abuse of children. I don't know if she read it or not. My father refused to even look at it. I wrote the poem "Refusal" to help myself understand that my father would never admit, say I'm sorry, nor come to terms with what he had done to me.

A year or so later, I was working at my computer. I saw her reflection in the monitor. At first, I thought it was me but the image was so much older. I wasn't thinking about her, but somehow my mind produced an image of her. One of my friends said she came back to see me. Since I have no idea what happens after death and I don't believe anyone else does, I assume that the image was produced in my mind.

Refusal

Communication is a road going everywhere.
Without it, the road goes nowhere.
I had a simple request
Read the book, restore the bond.
He refused!

The avenue for love, and trust is gone.
All I ever want is understanding,
All I ever get is denial.
The road has ended. It's blocked.
I have no desire to continue
For they have to meet me part way.

I can't read, learn or understand for them.
I can do no more.
My life's golden chariot beckons me.

I'll leave them behind.
Immersed in their misery.
No more will I bother,
For the rocky road of communication is closed.
I can go no further.

Barbara Weber   89

Through the Silk Screen of my Mind

I see a paintbrush wandering
Dripping with colors, drawing lines.
Images appear like no other
Through the silk-screen of my mind.

Purples of the universe
Blend with reds and whites of time.
Greens and yellows talk of earthly treasures.

While divine luminous spirits glide across the painting,
Completing the images I see
Through the silk-screen of my mind.

As I continued through therapy, I became more secure with my
creativity. I found that I enjoyed painting. I wrote to Paint a Symphony
expressing how I felt about the newly found freedom in using my creativity.

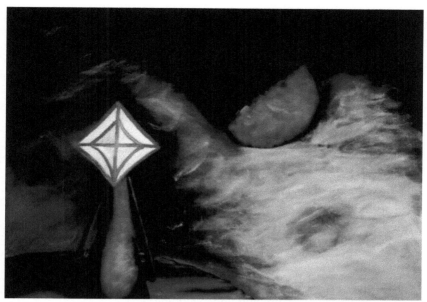

The Galaxy Surveyor (2004)

Galaxy surveyor represents a "higher being" watching over everything in the universe. I believe that I could disassociate during the events and according to Charlotte, that is what saved me.

The "Galaxy surveyor" looks through the looking glass making sure that all is going to plan. The purple planet is covered by clouds; the red planet of power is out of the clouds. Since I put myself in all of my paintings, I think both planets represent me. Although I am out of the clouds and empowered, an imprint of me remains in the clouds and influences my perspective on life.

My motivation and drive for healing came from my desire to do a superb job of raising my children. I had to work on me first. If I was to meet someone that would be good for me and be a good father for my children, I had to learn to like myself and eradicate my role of victim and improve my self-concept. If I decided to marry again, my children would be either positively or adversely affected. Thus, I entered therapy with a mammoth determination to change myself so that I would be able to have a healthy relationship with my children and any future husband.

As I finished therapy, I wrote: "who is this sitting in my chair?" Therapy had been successful, and I had transformed into a functioning woman.

Who?

Who is this person sitting in my chair?
She looks so familiar.
Do I speak to her?
I do not dare.
For she is a stranger
And has come from afar.

Do I greet her with warmth and understanding?
Do I shun and shame her away?
Is she friend or is she for?
I truly do not know!
Tell me, please, I care!
What do I say to this stranger
Sitting in my chair?

The Amulet of Love

The amulet of love
Enclosed by shimmering red, blue and purple glass.
Light and reflections harmonizing together singing the lullaby of love.

I want to be loved
Not because I can be used
But because of who I am
I want to proclaim
HERE I AM
DO YOU LOVE ME?

Barbara Weber   93

Love

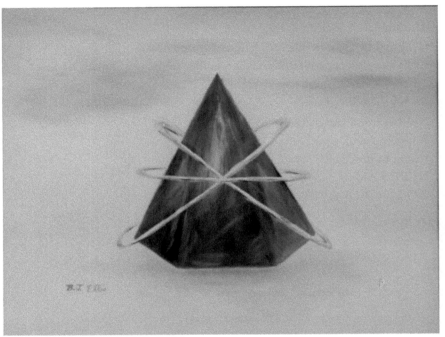

Love (1983)

This painting, if turned upside down, looks like a solitaire diamond. At the time I painted it, I didn't realize that fact. The rings surrounding the pyramid are like electrons spinning around an atom. Love is energy, delicate like glass and strong like a pyramid. The color of pink is soft and sensual. Purple represents the highest chakra, and the green represents healing.

This was my visual representation of love. I wanted to find someone to love who would be good for me. I also was looking for someone to love me back.

Clouds Parting

Clouds Parting (1983)

Barbara Weber 95

Shortly after my divorce, I dated men that were exactly like my ex-husband. It is said that unless we change the way we view ourselves we will attract the same kind of person as a lover repeatedly. I didn't like myself. Therefore, I attracted individuals who would treat me like I felt I should be treated — like crap. When with them, I reacted with what I called a plastic doll syndrome. I was like a plastic doll, I could be manipulated, and moved, however my partner wished. Once I began to change my attitude about myself, I attracted a different kind of man and the plastic doll syndrome eventually disappeared.

As I began to meet different kinds of men, I made a mental list of priorities that were important to me. What was I looking for in a man? I also realized that no one is perfect and as some characteristics became very important on my list, others were less important.

Going to singles mixers was a lot of fun for me. I drove myself there, danced and went home on my own. I began to meet men who treated me with respect and who seemed to be good men.

One of my students that I taught in the sixth grade would come down and talk, mow my lawn and help me do other yard work. His father had recently divorced, and he told me that his father was bringing home horrible women. I suggested that his father goes to one of the single mixers. I was going to one Friday night; I would meet him there. I would show him the ropes to being single.

His dad, Paul, met me there. I danced with him as well as with other men. I didn't know until later that he went to the mixer to be with me. I knew him professionally. I taught two of his boys and his wife taught my two children in preschool.

I had no intention of becoming involved with a newly divorced man because I felt that a man needs to "get his life together" so to speak after a recent separation or divorce.

We became good friends, then lovers and married the following spring. So much for allowing him time to "get his life together"! I tease him that he had to fill out a five-page application to marry me. In reality, I checked what characteristics I saw in him with my personal list of prioritized criteria of the man I wanted to marry. He was warm, soft, kind, had a good sense of humor and would give his shirt off his back for a friend. Above all, he was willing and seemed to be able to grow and change. I did not know at that time how important that attribute would be in the success of our marriage.

Before my husband and I married, I painted the "Clouds Parting" picture. The couple in front represented us. The clouds were parting with the dark clouds representing my past, the red clouds, the transition that I made during therapy and the yellow clouds represented a good future. The dark, gloomy days of the past were moving on, and my husband and I were looking toward a bright future, or so I thought.

To say the least, the first year was difficult. Two of his teenage boys lived with him and had been through two marriages. These were the two that I had taught in Elementary school. When we married, the third teenage boy requested to move in with us.

I knew adjustment would be difficult with this put-together family. But, I thought it would be easier since I had taught two of the boys in Elementary school. I was wrong. I found that the boys were not socialized. Paul raised them without any discipline or rules. The lack of a mother's love and care was evident. The boys noticed quickly how much my children had.

It really wasn't that they had a lot of toys or clothes but that they had a mother who gave them love, boundaries, and security. Paul had custody because their own mother seriously neglected them. He lost a court battle, and the eldest boy remained with his mother until Paul and I married.

My children inherited a dad, and Paul's boys were too old to respond to a strong women figure. I would take them shopping for school clothes, participate in school functions and go to their band concerts, but they wanted and needed more. With the changes going on in their minds and bodies, they were not receptive or even knowledgeable to what they needed.

At the beginning of the marriage, we all decided that Paul would not cook. I set up a physical loving home. In spite of that, the boys felt that they had lost their dad to my children and me. They were jealous, upset and reacted so. Periodically, as time progressed, there was a glimmer of hope. When Paul read a bedtime story to the younger children, the older boys would stop by the bedroom door, eventually, enter and sit on the bed to listen to the stories.

Not only did the boys have to deal with what they thought was competition, but Paul also changed the "rules of life." We were married one year when I was scheduled to go to a conference with a friend in San Francisco. Paul came home to drive me to the airport. However, I refused to get into the car because he was drunk. I called and canceled my flight. Paul was very upset, and we began to argue.

He stopped fighting and went upstairs. I fixed dinner.

The next day I took an airport shuttle and went to my conference. When I returned from the conference, I took my daughter to Girl Scout Camp and my son, and I went to our cabin. I wanted time to think. I couldn't believe that after all of the work I had gone through in therapy, I ended up marrying an alcoholic. There was no way I would continue to be married to Paul. I wouldn't put my children through that.

However, the following Wednesday, Paul called me. He told me he had joined AA and had not had a drink since I left. He couldn't understand that since he was taking care of the problem, why I wasn't coming home? I hung up and thought long and hard about it. Unwilling to keep my young children in a marriage where Paul was an alcoholic, I was ready to leave. However, there was something about the way he talked about taking care of the problem. He never said he was sorry, it wouldn't happen again. He took ownership of it. He took the first steps to become a recovering alcoholic. So I decided to take my son and go home.

It was easy for Paul to say the problem was solved. I know how difficult it is to change behavior. I could imagine that to stop drinking would require a lot of work and that it would not be easy to do. Besides, I heard the phrase, "I'll change, I promise," too many times.

He told me that the day when I refused to get into the car with him that he was headed toward the same kind of marriage he had before. He was forced to think that I would leave; which at that time was a very good possibility. His motivation to change came from the fact that he knew if he didn't stop drinking, he would eventually be alone, die drunk or end up in jail.

I had no idea as to how much he drank before this. Apparently, his day would begin at 6:00 A.M. with several beers. He would continue to drink all day long. Paul would drive with a beer can in his hand; when it was gone, he would stop and buy another one. I just didn't see it.

Paul continued to go to AA meetings, and we talked, and talked and talked. For a couple of years, I felt as if I was his therapist. He discussed his alcoholism with the boys, gave them the literature on ALANON and encouraged them to go to the meetings. He even took them to AA meetings. Most important, he quit drinking and has been dry for 31 years at the time of this writing.

Paul has been wonderful for my children. He has taught them to laugh, has been there for them, and has been a real steady influence on me. However, he is not perfect, and I am realistic in this matter. What really is pleasant is the fact that he doesn't expect me to be perfect either. We recognize our shortcomings. This makes our marriage strong.

Barbara Weber 99

She Bear

I a She-Bear stand tall and strong

The twinkle in my eye says it all.
No longer afraid of the Tiger
No longer afraid of the Wolf.
I greet each new day with a smile.

I am strong,
Not afraid to challenge life.
My day of freedom has come.
I am a survivor.

I had finished therapy. I felt strong and was sure that I had healed from my abuse. What I didn't know at the time was that abuse effects are lifelong. I had no idea of what that actually meant. I had heard that abuse victims have trouble trusting, but I was able to date men and eventually marry, so I thought I no longer had a problem.

At the time I finished therapy, the discussion of PTSD had just started in reference to men that returned from Vietnam. All of the talk in the media was about veterans having PTSD. I saw nothing about adult survivors of childhood sexual abuse connected to PTSD.

As far as I was concerned, I was healthy, happy and my children were growing up well adjusted. Boy was I ever wrong. Ramifications of childhood sexual abuse last the entire life of the survivor! I now know that from personal experience.

Barriers to Dreams

The grey bars on the picture, "Barriers to Dreams," represent the psychological barricades that I place between my desire to reach my dreams and the actual ability to achieve them. As depicted in the painting, my hurdles were solid iron bars strong enough to keep me from reaching my intellectual, creative goals and dreams. I was able to remove the barriers and can now take off in my hot air balloon toward the horizon. The horizon is far and vast. Dreams can be reached.

The valley is the road through which to travel. It is open with nothing to stop the balloons. As I sit in the yellow balloon, I can fly right up the valley toward the unknown and not be afraid. Nothing is stopping me.

Balance

Balance

I like putting geometrical shapes with organic shapes in my pictures. It's almost as if I'm painting sculptures, and I can feel the actual formation of the shapes. I call this picture balance because the ball is balancing in the air above the yellow shape. The ball represents life, the yellow shape is me. I'm sitting on a strong foundation represented by the heavy grey blocks and am now able to balance life. The flowers represent the beauty that surrounds me.

I thought I was balanced and ready to move forward in my life.

Companions

We called him Socks because he was all black, except for white around all four paws. The white extended a short distance up his legs making it look like he was wearing socks. I don't remember him as a puppy, so I have no idea how old he was when he used to walk in the woods with me.

Walking in the woods or forest has always been pleasant for me. I found out quickly as a child that I enjoyed taking off by myself on walks in the woods. Our house was surrounded by open areas with a lot of trees, animals and a train track.

Except for winter, I walked at every chance I got. Maybe it was to get away from home, maybe to just get away. Fall was my favorite season for walking. The trees were changing colors, and there was a hint of winter in the air. With my brother's hand-me-down short wool jacket and my jeans; Socks and I headed out and were often gone for several hours.

Sometimes I would walk along the train tracks. Socks had trouble walking on the trestle, so I avoided them. I have no idea how far I walked, I just walked until dusk, and I often met trains. One time, a train was closing in on me while I was on the tracks. I didn't have much time and was able to jump off the tracks to about two or three feet before the train passed. I could feel the pull of the train and thought I was going to be pulled under the train. I stopped walking down the tracks that day.

I have a picture of Socks and me when I was five. We are sitting on the porch of my next-door neighbor; Socks by my side. When we moved to the West Coast, we had to give him away to a farmer. Losing Socks, my friends, and moving was devastating to me. I hoped he was treated well by the farmer.

Many years later after I ended up in the hospital from reacting to a medication, I decided that if I was going to die, I was going to die happy. So, Paul and I purchased an American Eskimo puppy. She was white with black eyes, we named her Peppermint.

Barbara Weber   103

She was a good companion. We took her bike riding and hiking. We lived in Alaska at the time, and she was always good on the trail. One day she stopped and refused to go further. Hikers came toward us and told us that there was a bear near the trail not too far away. From then on, we never argued with Peppermint when she refused to continue a trail.

As Peppermint aged, we purchased a yellow carrier which attached to the back of Paul's bike. When Peppermint was tired and didn't want to run anymore, she climbed into the carrier and rode along with us. We rode many trails with Peppermint riding behind Paul.

At night when it was time to sleep, if Paul and I were talking or laughing, she would bark as if to say, it is time to go to sleep, stop messing around.

Peppermint had to be put down because she had cancer. She was thirteen years old; I lost a good friend. Someone who was always there, someone who made me feel good. A year after we put Peppermint down, we purchased Dugga, an Icelandic sheep dog.

In the morning, after we got up, she would jump on the bed, and use her paws and nose to move the pillow and the covers to make an open space. I guess she was airing out the bed. Dugga was always on duty making sure that she knew if either of us would leave the "den." She always knew where we were. Always one to travel, she loved to get into the car or motorhome. She never slept while we traveled. Instead she would sit and look out the window. When nearing the end of her life, we would put her in a wagon so she could participate in our walks with us.

When Dugga turned ten, she became very ill. The vet said she could have cancer or some other disease because her platelets were very high. After spending four months on medication, we had to put her down. I still miss her.

A year after purchasing Dugga, we bought Argo to be her companion. Argo is a dog with a personality that we have never seen a dog before. He talks to me, and I am sure he thinks I can understand him. Argo has not been trained to be a service dog, but he knows when I don't feel well, when I have a bad dream, or when I am depressed. Even at night if I am suicidal, he somehow knows. Jumping on the bed, he lies with his back to me, touching me. This calms me down and makes me feel better. During the day, if I don't feel well, he thinks that laying on my lap will make me feel better. Of course, a sixty-pound dog on my lap gets my attention. It is his way of telling me it is okay. Petting him is supposed to make me feel better as well.

Every morning I wake up and he is either next to me with his body touching me with his head on my pillow, or he is on the foot of the bed. Sometimes, I wake up and look over, and there are two brown eyes, two inches away from my face, looking at me. Once he sees me awake, his tail pounds the bed as it wags happily. If Paul gets up early and leaves the bed, Argo quickly moves to put his head on Paul's pillow. He makes himself right at home.

Before Dugga became so sick, both dogs would end up on the bed in the morning, one on one side of me and one on the other. We had to get a king-sized bed because there wasn't enough room for Paul, the two dogs and me.

We enjoy camping, and before Dugga became ill, we would take both dogs on the trails with us. Dugga was the boss and would bark when we stopped on the trail as if to say, "Why are you stopping? We are supposed to be walking!" Argo is the protector on a trail or just a walk around the block. I am supposed to be behind him. If I meander around and end up in front of him (as he stops to smell something), he will hit the back of my leg with his head or paw. That is his way of telling me to get behind him.

When I was waiting for Paul to sell our house, I was in one state, and he was in another. I had the dogs. They became my protectors. If Paul is fooling around or gets animated in telling me a story, Argo is right there between us. One time, we were laughing and fooling around. Paul took his hand and did a round swing at my arm. Argo was there immediately and grabbed his arm. I think that if I were in danger or was being harmed by a stranger, Argo would be right there to protect me.

My dogs have always helped me when I have been upset, hurt or ill. They have always been there for me. Their loyalty cannot be measured.

My Father's Death

When I was two years old, we moved to a university town in the Midwest. When I was in the sixth grade, we moved to California where my father obtained a job in a theater arts department at a college. After his arrest for the attempt to molest my younger sister's friend, he was asked to resign from his professorship.

This turned out to be a good move for him. He acquired another job in an industry that was at the forefront of entertainment. This gave him the opportunity to design many attractions that are known worldwide even today.

After retiring, he spent his time writing plays for theater and scripts for TV programs. He was always sending them out to agencies and each day he waited by the mailbox hoping for a chance to publish one of his plays. He had an unrealistic dream of being a famous playwright.

When I was in college, he asked me to read a couple of his plays. The dialog was full of profanity, the characters were flat without emotion, and the story (while maybe an interesting topic) never really went anywhere. I had no doubt that he would never publish any of his plays.

He was most interested in me reading one specific play. It was about a man that lived in a mental institution. He made friends with a little girl that would pass the institution while walking to and from school. He managed to get her to stop and talk to him. They became friends. I didn't like the story at the time, it gave me the creeps! To me it was an older male removing boundaries and seducing a little girl.

Maybe he thought he was mentally ill (he was), and maybe he thought he belonged in an institution. (He did). Since I never finished reading the entire script, I never asked him about it.

As he aged, he became active in the church again and wrote religious plays to be performed during various celebrations in the church. According to my older brother, they were successfully performed. He thought that my father was doing penance.

Dad died four years after my mother. Unable to function after she was gone, he was placed in an assisted living facility. I never visited him there. At the age of ninety-five, the family was all called (including me) to gather around and say goodbye to him as he was dying. Brothers, sisters, grandchildren, and great-grandchildren all made the journey, including my two children. I had no desire to fly down to see him, so I didn't go. I was the only relative that didn't say goodbye to him.

My daughter flew to California to say goodbye. In the hospital room, as she approached the bedside, she reached over to him and said, "Mom told me to tell you that she is sorry for not being here to say goodbye."

When she told me that, it made me angry. I was not sorry. I had no intention of "celebrating" his life at his funeral! My daughter's response was that he needed to hear that I had forgiven him. As far as I was concerned, I had forgiven him. I was no longer angry; I just didn't see any human connection between the two of us. To me, he was just some old man that I didn't know.

My father died the day he started molesting me.

Physical Illness

The physical and emotional stress of sexual abuse as a child places a great toll on the body of the child. This stress lasts as long as that person is alive. Survivors of childhood sexual abuse have a variety of profound physical illnesses as they age. If someone were to look at my medical history, and without knowing anything else about me, they would conclude that I had been sexually abused as a child. I had one doctor tell me that cellular memory never forgets. If I could figure out a way for me to use my mind to heal or change the cellular memory, it would be enormous.

When I was younger, I had allergies, but they were never life-threatening. As I entered my mid-forties, I became more sensitive and had several anaphylactic episodes. During this time, I was at the dentist. He used a latex rubber dam across my mouth when filling a tooth. I started wheezing and became quite congested. Not understanding what was happening, I got up to leave. The dentist asked me if I was alright. My go-to response when asked if I am alright, is to always say, "Yes, I am ok." Since I had no idea what was going on with me, I left the office.

I don't understand why he allowed me to leave. Aren't dentists schooled in allergic reactions? After hopping in my car and turning the corner to go home, I realized that I couldn't breathe. Since my primary physician's office was around the corner from the dentist, I turned into the parking lot and parked my car. As I walked into the office, the receptionist took one look at me and took me back to a treatment room. My doctor came in, started an IV with some sort of medication and gave me a breathing treatment. After a few hours in his office, he allowed me to go home.

Worried about my allergies, after the episode at the dentist office, my primary doctor thought it would be a good idea to do skin testing on me, telling me that he thought desensitization shots would help. As he was using needles with the allergens (weeds, trees, and grasses) under my skin, my hands turned red and itched. Miserable, drowning from the inside and unable to tolerate the itching hands, I shrieked "My hands are itching." Ice packs were useless, they didn't help. I passed out. I only remember a paramedic introducing herself. The next thing I knew it was several hours later and I woke up in the ER. Apparently, the paramedics needed to intubate me because they thought I was going to stop breathing. By the time I woke up, I was no longer intubated. Paul was at the ER when the ambulance brought me in. He didn't think it was me on the gurney because it didn't look like me. I was lifeless, grey and swollen. He said I looked like a giant hive.

This was the start of my severe reactions to environmental stimuli and drug therapies. I think it has something to do with the touch of a foreign or unwanted object. If I encounter something I am allergic to, my immune system thinks it is an enemy and reacts with an army to protect me. There is some research to back that up. One of the reasons why sexual abuse of a very young child is so devastating to the child is because it involves touch.

A couple of years later, my husband cleaned the bathroom with a chemical. He left to go to a meeting. However, I noticed the smell and realized it bothered me, so I went in and mopped the entire bathroom with clean water. Finished, I walked out to the hallway and apparently passed out on the floor of the bedroom. I must have yelled for my son, and he called 911. I woke up at some point, and the paramedic told me that when he came in, my face was bright red. He asked what had happened. I told him about the chemical in the bathroom and that I had cleaned it. I passed out again. The only memory I have of that night was someone rubbing something on my breastbone and telling me to stay with them. My breastbone area was incredibly sore the next day. I had had a severe allergic reaction.

Even reactions from medications cause me to go into anaphylaxis. Morphine closes my throat, and I reacted to a dental mouthwash after having a dental implant procedure completed. Not feeling well, I went to the ER. Throwing up black coffee-like material, I was immediately moved to the treatment area. As the nurse was waiting for me to be moved upstairs to intensive care, she told me that I was looking sicker and sicker in front of her eyes. I am not sure that was the right thing to tell me.

According to the doctor, the mouthwash causes one percent of the population to have a bleeding stomach. He also told me that I needed to do something, move out of where I was living because if I go into anaphylaxis again, he might not be able to pull me out without adverse side effects.

My husband and I moved to Alaska which had cleaner air and fewer pollens to worry about. I was so much better. It helped with my day to day allergy relief, but that didn't stop my allergic reactions. Years later, I had reconstructive knee surgery. The doctors gave me morphine for pain in the recovery room, and my throat closed. They moved quickly to counter the reaction, and I was given a list of allergens that I needed to put on a medic alert card.

Since then the list of medications that I am allergic to or have had an adverse reaction to has grown exponentially; I also have been tested for food allergies, and the list is huge. I used to hear that a child who has been sexually abused will be affected all of their life. I always thought that since I successfully completed therapy in my thirties, my abuse wouldn't impact me my entire life. I was wrong. It took me until I was seventy before I got any relief from PTSD. My allergies remain more intense. Currently, I have severe environmental and food allergies.

I am unable to go to concerts, weddings or funerals because of the enormous probability of sitting next to or passing someone with perfume or who is a smoker and because weddings and funerals have flowers. Both perfume and smoke (even on clothing) cause me to wheeze and to develop an instant allergic migraine. Flowers are also a problem. Many flowers have added perfume which makes them very aromatic. Even if the perfume isn't added, I can't be anywhere near them inside a building.

When Paul and I are out in public, and we enter a building and notice construction or an odor, we leave. Too many times I have tried to stay and have had serious allergic reactions.

Before moving to this community, Paul and I drove up to look at houses. We were looking for an inexpensive house because I was going to stay a year or so while Paul tried to sell our home in another state. As the realtor took us around, I would walk into these older homes, some completely remodeled, and start to wheeze. It was worse when I went down into basements. I can walk into any home and tell right away if there is mildew or mold somewhere in the home because I will immediately wheeze and have an allergic reaction. I also found that I couldn't walk into a home that had new carpet because the off-gassing of chemicals made me instantly ill.

After three or four houses, we walked into a more expensive home. I had no trouble. The realtor decided that if we were going to spend that much on an old home, it would be better to purchase a newly built home for the same price. That worked out fine. I moved into a home that was set up for me.

A year later, Paul joined me. Again, we went out to look at a larger home. The first house we saw had brand new carpet. The fumes were intolerable. I held my breath and ran through the layout of the house to see if I liked it. That was all it took. As we drove to another home, I sat in the back and realized that I was having trouble swallowing. Embarrassed and not willing to stop the process of looking for houses; (after all the realtor had planned to spend an entire day with us), I took four Benadryl.

When we came to the next house, I didn't get out and look. I decided to stay in the car. The sensation of not being able to swallow came back. I took more Benadryl. We ended up looking at houses half a day. When I got home, I took my nebulizer and some prednisone. The next day, I went to see my primary physician and told him what happened to me. He said that I needed to call 911 or I would be a corpse in the back seat.

I had another serious reaction and didn't call 911. When I saw my doctor, my lungs were damaged, and I was having difficulty breathing. He took an x-ray of my chest and gave me prednisone and a cough medication to stop the spasms in my lungs. Concerned that I didn't call 911 for help when I desperately need to call them, I asked him how I could be able to call for help. He referred me to the psychiatrist Gabriella that was working in the medical clinic at the time.

I saw Gabriella within a couple of weeks. She asked me some questions at the beginning of the visit. These were questions that didn't bring up any memories of the past but helped narrow down why I was there. Gabriella's explanation to me as to why I don't call for help was that because I was abused, I am used to handling trauma on my own. I hide and manage my problems myself. I had asked for help from my mother, from the nurse at school and the psychologist at college and didn't get any. Because I didn't get help from any of them, I now do not ask for it. The ramifications of childhood abuse never goes away.

She suggested a cognitive cue to tell me to call for help. It will also help my husband determine when to call. I am now wearing a watch that also monitors my heart rate. If I start having an allergic reaction and my heart rate goes above 130, I am to call 911. I have been unable to use the cognitive cue.

Barbara Weber   111

That doesn't mean I haven't had any problem in which 911 should have been called. A year ago, I lost my balance and fell backward in a parking lot. I landed first on my left hand, my right, and hit my head and was knocked out. Paul helped me up, I don't remember anything until I was standing and said I was ok.

Since I hit my head, I wasn't able to determine how badly I was hurt. I broke my wrist, ruptured the bicep tendons in both arms and had a concussion. It turns out that I lack a protein to absorb vitamin B12 and because of that, I wasn't able to control my right leg and have been losing my balance for years. A year later, I was still recovering from the injuries received on that day. Paul is angry at himself for not calling 911. My attitude is that nothing has changed. I doubt if I will call the next time I need help. I just don't.

I don't even ask for help in the doctor's office. I went to see my heart doctor because I was having some trouble. When I walked out of the examination room, I fell over and caught myself on the reception counter. The receptionist asked if she should call the doctor. "No, I said." I didn't ask for help. After several tests, it turns out that I have a rare arrhythmia and need to take two heart medications to control it.

Not asking for help started a long time ago. When I was six, I was waiting outside after school for someone to pick me up. I stood for a while watching older kids jump off the top of the cement stairs to the bottom, and it looked like fun. I tried it. I landed funny and broke my ankle. Did I ask for help then? No. I went back up the stairs into the schoolhouse. I turned to the right and walked past the principal's office.

Further down, I passed the nurses office. Because the school had k-6 on one end and 7-12 on the other, the hallway joining the sections was quite long. I entered the "forbidden" 7-12 grade section and kept walking. Several students stopped to see if they could help. Crying I said "no" and kept walking. I walked out the end door and down the steps. I was on my way to the theater arts building across campus. I walked quite a distance to a tunnel that went under the street. After I came out of the tunnel, I still had quite a way to go walking on a broken ankle. Once I made it to Elmer's office, he put me in the car and took me to the ER. I sported a white plaster cast and was on crutches for six weeks.

I have since figured out that there are two reasons why I don't ask for help. The first reason is that I tend to "tough it out," so to speak. I manage on my own. This comes from when I was three and had to deal with dizzy spells on my own.

I also am afraid of asking for medical help when I need it because there may be nothing wrong. This came from when I went to visit the gynecologist in college because I had pain in my abdomen. Instead of helping me, he assaulted me.

I have gone to the gym regularly since I was in my early thirties, eaten properly, taken care of myself and I still have some very serious physical troubles. Stress takes a toll on the body. Stress from PTSD is no different. My physical problems are acerbated from stress.

Compliance Vs. Willingness

After the gynecologist assaulted me when I was in college, I never went back to one for a check-up or for routine care. My primary physician prescribed birth control pills for me. At twenty-eight, I was pregnant, I needed to see an OB/GYN and followed medical advice until I gave birth. Two years later, I was pregnant again with my son. I again visited the OB/GYN. I hemorrhaged after giving birth, and the doctor told me no more children. After a year of very heavy two-week periods, I had a hysterectomy. That ended my visits to the OB/GYN.

Most of my doctors have been male. I have no problem going to the doctor for colds, etc. I get extremely nervous when I have to go for surgery or anything that requires more than a normal exam.

I have had many skeletal surgeries in my life. I hurt my knees in college and tore my cruciate ligament after tripping over a tombstone. Surgery always makes me anxious. What escalates my anxiety is when the individuals in the OR start prepping me for the surgery without putting me under first. My wrists have been tied down and my face covered (I can't see what they are doing). To my way of thinking, this takes away my power; my ability to defend myself, even though in reality I won't have to defend myself, I still feel the loss of power. As a result, I have difficulty controlling my anguish. I never say anything and instead deal with it internally, causing tremendous distress.

Recently, I have had several other medical procedures. In one case, I had a loop recorder placed under my skin on my chest. The doctor was late so the personnel in the OR tied my wrists down and started covering my face in anticipation of the doctor's arrival. Here, I was able to say something about being a sexual abuse survivor. I couldn't see what they were doing. I said something about being a sexual abuse survivor. The anesthesiologist immediately put me under. Sometime in the future, I am going to have to go in and have the loop recorder removed. When the doctor says it is time to have it removed, I will comply, however difficult that will be. I hope I can tell the nurse that is getting me ready to go into the procedure to have them wait until I am out to prepare me.

The only time I felt relaxed when having a procedure or surgery was when I had a colonoscopy. Since I avoided the procedure all my life, Dr. Stevenson referred me to a female gastroenterologist. I was seventy years old when I went in for the procedure. There were only women in the OR waiting for me. With a female doctor as well, this was the most successful procedure, as far as I was concerned, that I have ever undergone. I was relaxed from the minute they wheeled me into the OR. I won't have any difficulty going back for the procedure.

In my life, I have been transported to the ER several times. Most of the time I was in anaphylaxis. However, I passed out (once when camping), fell and hit my head and was also transported to the ER. A male nurse came in to take care of me. The male nurse started to undress me. Realizing that if I didn't say anything, I was going to get up and leave even though I was badly hurt (I had broken a rib, suffered a concussion and needed stitches), I said something to the effect that I was a survivor and I wanted a female nurse.

He went to get a female nurse for me, which meant that she and he had to exchange patients and he had to walk from one section to another. Looking at his face and his body language, I got that he wasn't happy. There was no way I was going to be compliant with him.

The medical group where I see my doctors has a hospital. Recently, I was there overnight. I have anxiety listed on my chart and am asked about it every time I go to the ER. Anxiety is the code word for someone who has PTSD. While staying overnight at the hospital, a medical professional of some sort came into my room (around eleven PM). He said he needed to add some missing information to my admission paperwork. I guessed that he was a psychologist just by the way he walked into the room. (He bounced with each step and had an air of confidence).

After asking me a mixture of questions about what kind of electronic and personal items I had, he asked me about my anxiety. I questioned him if he meant my PTSD? He answered yes. I said that I was no longer experiencing PTSD symptoms such as walking in my sleep or having nightmares. I was nervous about staying overnight in the hospital, however.

After a few minutes, he directed our conversation to what I do to relax. I

Barbara Weber 115

replied that my husband and I go camping and hiking. There is something about walking among the old growth forest that makes me feel good. I said my favorite place to camp and hike was the Olympic Peninsula.

I began to relax when thinking about walking through the trees. I guess he felt that I was getting tired, he got up to leave and turned the light off. I put my head down and felt him standing over me. I could see his hand held out to shake my hand. I saw the hand and said, "Oh, okay," I figure that he was trying to get me to trust him and show me that I was safe in the hospital. My primary physician once told me that I didn't trust him. He also shook my hand each time I left his office as well. I think it was a way in which to get me to trust a male medical professional.

I understand the need for me to have less anxiety while in the ER or the hospital. If I have a serious problem, the doctors need to be concerned about saving my life rather than about my feelings of mistrust and insecurity which can lead to difficulties in accessing what is medically wrong with me.

The Beginning of the End

If someone were to meet me as I worked and raised my children, they probably would not have realized that I was suffering from the sexual abuse that I had experienced as a child. It wasn't until I was sixty-six years old that a doctor, after hearing about my difficulties sleeping, told me I had PTSD (Post Traumatic Stress Disorder). I always thought that it was a terrible syndrome that was common among combat veterans.

To be fair, it wasn't until the 1980s that PTSD was first acknowledged. By that time, I was in my late thirties and had finished therapy. I don't believe that it was fully investigated until the 1990s where it was determined that anyone who encounters a trauma can develop PTSD. I am not surprised that when I would mention my difficulties in sleeping that no doctor ever mentioned that I had PTSD.

Paul was in Wyoming trying to sell our house as a short sale. It was on the market for three years. The downturn in 2008 made it difficult a difficult sale. I had to move because I needed oxygen at the 6400 feet elevation where we had lived. I don't need it at lower levels.

Lonely, I would sit and read all day. I ended up reading a book a day and ate a bag of bite-sized Snickers almost every day. As a result, I gained 35 pounds in less than nine months. When Paul joined me, I decided to try to lose the weight. I had seen advertisements for a group called "Positive Changes." This wasn't a diet plan but used hypnotherapy to help people lose weight. I enrolled in a sixth-month plan to lose weight.

At the time of my intake interview with "Positive Changes," I mentioned that I was a survivor of childhood sexual abuse. I was set up with my first meeting with a counselor. The interview lasted an hour. I mentioned my sexual abuse, and we talked about what reasons I have for overeating. At my first appointment, they made a personal recording for me. I sat in a recliner with dark glasses that had a strobe light that blinked at a rapid rate while I was listening to the tape. They also gave me two introductory CDs.

My instructions were for me to come to the office twice a week to listen to pre-recorded CDs for half an hour and meet in a group for another half an hour with one of their personnel. I also was to listen to the personal and general CDs two or three times a day. I listened in the morning and in the evening. Sometimes I listened at noon as well.

Each month I got a new personalized recording to listen to. At the end of six months, I had lost thirty pounds and have continued to lose an additional twenty pounds. The group has a plethora of other specific CDs available for purchase. I was having chronic pain in my shoulder, so I purchased a CD for chronic pain. I didn't realize that the CD deals with emotional pain and engages the brain as a pharmacy to heal the body. I listen to that CD for over a year. I also received other benefits from the program.

It took more than six months to stop the nightmares, sleep walking, and reacting to triggers. I still had one last struggle before closure. One and a half years before successfully closing the door on my abuse, I was training my dog, Argo. I had his leash around my waist, and it was attached to Argo's collar. Losing my balance, I fell backward like a tree (Argo anchored the leash, so it didn't move) and braced my fall first with my right hand and then my left. Hitting my head on the pavement followed. It was a terrible fall. I ended up breaking the Scaphoid bone in my wrist and suffering a concussion.

Because of the concussion, my migraines became so frequent and were so painful that I had difficulty functioning. To get rid of the migraines, I took a lot of medication. Eventually, my neurologist obtained permission from the insurance company to do a Botox treatment every 12 weeks. He also prescribed an infusion of Sodium Medrol which made a difference in the number and intensity of migraines.

Six months after I fell, I was still having pain in my shoulder. I went to see Dennis, a Physician's Assistant, about the pain in my arm. He had been administering shots in my knees every six months in the hopes that I could avoid knee replacement surgery. At the time, I thought he was an MD. He never said he was, but he never corrected me either.

"Hello, Barbara. Why are you here?" he remarked as he walked through the exam door.

"Remember, I fell a few months ago, and my arm hasn't stopped hurting," I said, pointing to the place where I hurt.

"What do you want me to do about it?" He sat across from me.

Not too sure how to respond to that comment, I said nothing.

He stood up, measured the strength of my arm. "Move your arm this way," moving his arm out, then made a funny loop with it. He left the room.

"I ordered an MRI for you." He said when he came back into the room.

Office visit over, I left. As I walked downstairs, anger spread throughout my entire core. I felt degraded, devalued and humiliated. He didn't take me seriously. He didn't listen to me!

The anger was like a ball rolling down a hill. Unable to sleep, I decided to never go back to him for anything. Unfortunately, I had to see him in a week for biannual shots in my knees. Fuming, I thought, "*That will be the last time I see him. I will also tell him how unprofessional he was toward me. I will tell him how I feel.*"

When he first walked into the room on the day I was to get my shots in my knees, I said, "We need to talk."

"Sure."

"I didn't appreciate the way you spoke to me and treated me at my last visit. I felt that you degraded, devalued and humiliated me. You didn't take me seriously, and you didn't listen to me."

"I am sorry," he moved closer to me and placed his hand on my knee.

As soon as his hand touched my knee, I heard a swooshing sound as I felt something (I guess it was me) leave my feet and hands and end up at the far upper back of the right side of my head. There I was, the size of a pin tip. I was looking down at my hands through the bony eye sockets of my skull. My ice-cold hands in my lap seemed small. I flashed back to when I was 13 and the junior high school nurse was sitting across from me.

•   •   •   •   •

"There is nothing wrong with you. You are not ill," she chastised. "You have come in here too often complaining that you are sick."

She isn't letting me say anything. She is just yelling. My period started. I am afraid I could become pregnant. If she would just shut up and listen, I could tell her.

• • • • •

Dennis seemed far away, even though he was only sitting four feet from me. His voice muffled. I have no idea what he was saying. I came back into the room; not sure how long I was disassociated. When I came through the garage door into the house, Paul noticed that something was wrong with me. He gave me big hug. It took several hours for me to return to myself again.

I wrote a note to the CEO of the medical health care provider. I told them that the Physician's Assistant degraded, devalued and humiliated me at an office visit. I also mentioned that I had disassociated when he leaned forward and touched my knee. The medical provider needed to do some personnel training on PTSD.

I never had the MRI. I waited for another three months before I sought help for the excruciating pain in my arm. I made an appointment to see another physician's assistant named Ron. I opted to see a physician's assistant because I could get in to see them faster than an MD. After an examination of my arm, he determined that I had done something to my bicep tendon. He wanted to do an ultrasound-guided cortisone shot. Before he could do the procedure, he needed to obtain permission from my insurance.

We discussed pain medication. He said he would write a prescription for me. It would be at the front of the office.

After leaving the office, I thought that I didn't want anything to do with Ron. The similarities between Ron and Dennis were too much; both male, similar procedures, both Physician's Assistants. I couldn't sleep. All I could think about is that there is no way Ron was going to touch me. At 9:00 the next morning, I called his office and asked that the request for insurance approval be canceled.

Apparently, they had already sent the request to my insurance company because an office worker called me that afternoon to tell me that the procedure had been approved. They wanted to know what day would be best for me to come in for the procedure. After deciding to not have the procedure, I told them I would call back. I had planned to never call them back. Although the two medical professionals were not the same, they both were physician assistants, and both did guided ultra-sound injections.

I was more upset about having Ron do a procedure on me than I realized. Saturday night after the office visit, I woke Paul pounding my fists into the nightstand next to my side of the bed. I hit it with first one hand and then the other. Repeatedly, I pummeled the table. Awakened with a start, Paul reached over from his side of the bed and struggled to grab hold of my arms. First one arm and the next. He couldn't get a hold of either arm. I continued to hammer the table. Minutes passed. I continued to thrash.

Eventually, he managed to wrap his arms around me and held me tight. After a few minutes, I stopped; I never woke up. I knew nothing of the incident until the next morning.

Monday came around and no medication, so I called the office. I spoke with a nurse and asked if the pain medication prescription had been written. I said that it felt like I had a hot piece of metal, poking my arm. I also mention that I thought I had broken my hand. She made an appointment for the afternoon for me to see the hand doctor. She called me back when she couldn't find a prescription for me.

"You know," she said. "This is an orthopedic office. We handle only orthopedic injuries. The hot pain you are feeling may be nerve pain, and you should see another office."

I hung up. Her statement made me extremely angry. I called back, spoke to the office staff and canceled my appointment with the hand doctor. "If they refuse to help me, I will manage the pain myself!"

The next morning, Ron's assistant called me at home and told me the pain prescription was at the front desk. The doctor was in surgery on Friday, and they both had the day off on Monday. I told her of my experience with the nurse and that I think I had broken something in my hand. I can't believe how emotional I was. I was angry. I was sobbing. The assistant told me that Ron would take care of my hand. I said I would wait.

The pain in my hand was excruciating. Calling up the assistant the next morning, I made an appointment to see Ron.

It had been five days since I pounded the end table when I saw Ron. Water poured out of my eyes. I had lost all capability of being balanced. Crying inconsolably, I whispered to Ron, "I tried so hard... It is unbelievably painful." After the X-rays, Ron showed me on the X-ray where I had broken my thumb. "How did you do this?"

"I had a PTSD episode," I mumbled.

Two hours later, blue cast on my hand and wrist, I walked out of the office. A week later, I went back for a guided ultrasound cortisone injection in my bicep tendon.

Apparently, both the CEO of the Health provider and the orthopedic office notified my primary physician, Dr. Stevenson, about my dissociation and eventual breaking of my thumb during a PTSD episode. When I called to make an appointment, I was surprised that I got in to see him the next day. I had no idea that Dr. Stevenson was on medical leave after having back surgery. He came into the office to see me three weeks from having the surgery.

Walking into the room stiffly, Dr. Stevenson sat down in a chair where his knee almost touched mine. He put the laptop down on a small table to the left of me.

"Why are you so stiff. Is something wrong?" I asked.

"I had back surgery three weeks ago."

"Then why are you here seeing me? Why are you at work?"

"Barbara, I am very concerned about you. How do I know if you dissociate with me?

"I would never dissociate with you because you don't talk to me the way Dennis did. You always treat me with respect, and you always listen to me. I would never do that to you."

Dr. Stevenson wrote something down on his laptop.

I continued, "When I told Dennis that my arm hurt, he said what do you want me to do about it? I felt degraded, devalued and humiliated. He didn't take me seriously nor did he listen to me. He triggered me. You don't talk to me that way!"

I resumed my explanation. "I disassociated and flashed back to when I was thirteen and in the school nurse's office. I had started my menses. Even though the molestation had stopped, I was terrified that I'd become pregnant. I went to the nurses' office often. I am not certain how many times I visited, but it was enough for her to ball me out. To tell me that there was nothing wrong with me and I needed to stop going to her when there was nothing wrong."

Dr. Stevenson maintained his concentration and typed everything that I was saying down on his laptop.

I continued, "Because I was sexually abused until I was 10 or 11, at 13 I was worried about getting pregnant. I didn't know sperm live for only three days."

"When did the abuse end?"

"It lasted until I was ten."

Dr. Stevenson changed the subject. "How can I tell if you dissociate?"

"I don't know. Maybe I would be distant, not in the same room with you. My degree is in Educational Psychology. Ask a professional in the field." I was getting testy.

Changing the subject again, he nodded at my cast.

"I had a PTSD episode. I pounded the table next to my bed and ended up breaking my thumb. I have no idea what I was dreaming."

"Did you wake up?" He asked.

"No."

He didn't say anything, so I resumed. "I have had PTSD all of my life. I have walked in my sleep since I was six. I had dizzy spells with the room spinning since I was three. At sixteen, I managed to figure out a way to stop the room from spinning. I would wake up screaming that there is a man in the room standing by my bed. My husband (sometimes yelling my name) would say that there was no one there, but I insisted. I could even describe what the man was wearing. I have dreams where men, aliens and/or horses are chasing me. One time I woke up with the phone in my hand because some green Martians were chasing me. Apparently, I tried to call 911. I am so glad they didn't answer. It's funny now."

"It isn't funny."

"It is. Can you imagine if the 911 operator answered and I said that six green Martians are chasing me?"

"It isn't funny!" He said with indignation.

"One time, six years ago, I was dreaming that men were coming after me and I needed to hide. Apparently, I walked into my home office, went from a standing position to sitting (I woke up when my butt hit the floor), fell back, hit my head on the wall and knocked myself out. The dog woke me up licking my face. I have no idea how long I was out. I went back to bed, but the next morning I had to go to the ER because my headache was terrible. I had a concussion and spent the following week in bed unable to sit up because every time I did, I got sick to my stomach and dizzy."

Dr. Stevenson was busy typing everything that I was saying.

I continued, "I didn't know my dreams and walking in my sleep were PTSD until I saw you for the first time. You told me I had PTSD. Every doctor I have seen all my life, I told them that I walked in my sleep. They always told me to make sure I was safe. I guess a concern was that I would walk out the front door in -20-degree weather. I always thought that only veterans had PTSD. That is all I have ever heard about."

"You didn't know you had PTSD?"

"No, not until you said something about it four years ago when I first saw you."

When Dr. Stevenson mentioned that I had PTSD, I had a name for my problems at night and for flashbacks or triggers that I occasionally experienced. Up until that time, I always thought that PTSD was what veterans get. There is so much talk about the effects of war on men and women. Many commit suicide, many are homeless. I have functioned for years, have always worked and have a family life.

I continued, Dr. Stevenson proceeded to type. "I was sexually abused from the age of 5 (I think) until the age of 10. I remember one incident when I was 5 or 6 and remember the last incident. I remember nothing in between. I had intense therapy for 3 years and went back when I would have flashbacks. However, I remember at the age of 3, when put down for a nap, I would start screaming that my hand was caught in the door and the room was spinning. I remember screaming, and my mother would come in and tell me that my thumb was not in the door and to go to sleep. I stopped yelling. Dr. Carlson, my therapist, thought that the sexual abuse started when I was three. I don't know. I don't remember any trauma that would cause me to see my hand caught in the door.

"Afterward, every night when I went to sleep, I would wake up with the room spinning around me. This lasted until I was 16. One night I was able to stop the room from spinning. I have no idea how I did it.

Dr. Stevenson looked at me. "I am really worried about you. I want to refer you to a Psychiatrist."

To me it was no big thing. I have struggled with PTSD all my life. However, I had never dissociated as an adult before, and I had never disassociated because of a flashback or trigger to something that happened to me as a child. I agreed to see someone.

Dr. Lee

At the first meeting with Dr. Lee, he asked me a plethora of questions, one of which was if I had ever tried to commit suicide. At the time he asked that, I answered, "No." However, the next day I remember that I had tried to commit suicide when I was twenty-three. Remembering that flashbacked to the time that I attempted to take my life. I felt all of the emotions of that time rush back into me. I slid into the black abyss next to me on my right side. I regretted not being successful in taking my life. This time I decided to make sure that I would be successful. I made a plan of taking leftover pain pills that I had in surgery a few months before. Oxycodone makes me ill so I didn't take them. When I went around the house, I found other pain pills from other surgeries. It was enough to guarantee success. I thought about this obsessively. I couldn't get it out of my mind. I had a plan and was going to guarantee that it would work. I eventually threw the pills away.

Despite my determination and well laid out plans, I had my seventieth birthday. That morning my daughter and her two children SKYPED me from France. The kids sang happy birthday to me in English, French, and Italian. They laughed and giggled, and I enjoyed seeing and listening to their stories. The kids call me regularly before they go to bed and my daughter often calls me after putting them to bed. I enjoy those calls.

Later that afternoon, my son called me. His two children and wife were out of the country visiting their other grandparents. He is busy with work and his family, but he always finds time to call me on special holidays and my birthday. Sometimes, he just calls to talk.

That evening, Paul surprised me with a pink and white decorated ice cream birthday cake and a card. I felt myself moving out of the abyss. I wasn't completely out and back to normal, but as usual, my children, grandchildren, and husband made me feel better. We went camping afterward, and that put me back to normal where the thought of suicide was buried deep inside.

During my life, I have made one attempt at suicide and was suicidal two other times besides the one just discussed. After a couple of years of my first marriage, I realized that I had made a huge mistake. I was trapped. No one cared about me, and I cared about no one. One evening after enduring a barrage of criticisms, I took a brand-new full bottle of both Tylenol and aspirin (that is everything that I had in the medicine cabinet). All that did was become very ill.

I was scheduled for one more visit with Dr. Lee. I decided that he triggered me into a depressive state by asking me about suicide attempts. I didn't like the idea of him sitting behind his huge desk and attempting to get me to open up about deeply important issues. Psychiatric help was not what I needed, although I wasn't sure what it was that I did need to come to closure.

On the day of my scheduled visit with Dr. Lee, I went in with the intention of never seeing him again. I told him about my suicide thoughts, how compulsive they were and how they interrupted every thought and action. He agreed that he wasn't going to open the Pandora's Box. He did check to make sure that I had come out of my depression enough that I wouldn't be a danger to myself, and then I left. I hadn't completely closed the book on my life of PTSD.

A Tiger in the Yard

I painted this tiger, at the beginning of my therapy, as a leopard. I had no idea that it was a leopard. I guess I didn't really look at it. When my daughter was an adult, I was explaining the emotion behind the scene. She pointed out that the tiger was a leopard. I added stripes at that time but left the face alone.

The painting is of the house that I lived in when I was five, and the abuse began. It serves as a warning that children should not come into the yard. A tiger lives there and preys upon little children. He is all-powerful, controlling, fierce, frightening and treacherous.

The turned-over wagon is used by the tiger as a place to hide. In other words, the tiger knows just what to do to maneuver little girls into his lair. The house has some three-dimensionality, but the flowers and plants along the side of the house are flat and look painted on. They don't look real. There is no feeling in the house, no emotions. There is a welcome mat, but danger lurks for any little girl that enters.

After reading my manuscript, Paul thought he would purchase a shirt with a tiger on it for me. He remembered that I wanted to purchase a shirt at a Yosemite gift shop when I was married to my first husband. I picked the shirt out, and Abani said loudly for others to hear, "You are not getting that shirt. You are no tiger!"

Paul thought it would be wonderful if he got a shirt as a surprise. I opened the package, and to my surprise, a tiger stared at me. Terror ran down to my core. I quickly turned it over on the sofa so I wouldn't have to look at it.

Trying to ignore the shirt, I went into the kitchen to fix dinner. As I worked, I wondered why a picture of a tiger would scare me so much. It seemed silly to me that I didn't like the picture. During the evening, I went back and looked at the shirt a couple of times. Each time I picked the shirt up, my fear lessened. Finally, looking at this innocuous picture no longer frightened me. It was at that time; I knew I needed to do something. I needed to...

Face the tiger.

Barbara Weber   129

Closure

I am finally healed from years of suffering from symptoms of PTSD. It took me two years to realize that I no longer had nightmares or walked in my sleep. We had purchased a new home with our master bedroom on the second floor. Paul put an alarm on the bedroom door so that if I walked, it would buzz and wake me up. We were afraid that I would fall down the stairs. Instead, the alarm never sounded. I was no longer walking in my sleep. It was then that I realized that I wasn't having nightmares anymore either. What helped me heal was a "group effort," so to speak. I needed therapy, the help of my primary physician and my husband.

Even though I no longer experience nightmares, sleepwalking at night and triggers during the day, depression raises its ugly head often. I have been diagnosed with Complex PTSD caused by long-term trauma such as years of sexual abuse. My struggle with many issues seems to have no end. I have achieved tremendous success in overcoming issues from abuse and eliminating PTSD symptoms. Symptoms of Complex PTSD have not gone away. I have one last struggle, and with the help of a therapist, I should succeed in overcoming it.

Where is the Little Girl Years Later?

After healing from the abuse and PTSD, I decided to paint another picture of the church titled "Where is the Little Girl?". Here I painted the picture as a fall picture. The church is old and abandoned. The doll still rests where the little girl once placed her for safe keeping. She is a symbol of my lost childhood and the abuse. I have no need to retrieve her.

Where is the Little Girl?

Barbara Weber   131

Because of Others

Sometime after approaching my mother for the first time about my abuse, she gave me a picture frame that she had made from plastic canvas. She used pink yarn to weave in and out to cover the plastic. In the upper right-hand corner, she placed two silk flowers and a silk ribbon box in the center.

Inside the frame, she typed "Love is the way." It meant nothing to me at the time. I scoffed at it and said out loud, "What does she know about love?" I threw it into a drawer. For years, I never paid any attention to the framed saying. I am not certain why I didn't lose it in my many moves. I came across it after painting the tiger. I had placed it with my photos. The frame sits on my desk, with "love is the way" typed on a now yellowed piece of paper.

When it came to touch, I never felt the warm embrace of love. When it came to touch from my husband, I always connected that with sexual arousal. After facing and painting the Tiger, I have a different feeling when I hug my husband, or he hugs me. I can feel his love, and I can express it. Maybe it has something to do with making peace with myself or making peace with the controlling tiger that held me captive for all these years. I am now finally free of his power.

After I wrote the poem "Because of Others," I looked at the last line and couldn't make sense as to why I wrote, "I am loved." I changed it to "I am victorious," and "I have succeeded." Neither one of those made any sense. No, I wanted "I am loved" to be the last line. After thinking about it for some time, I realized that what this means to me is that I can feel the love in Paul's touch.

Because of Others

Celebrating a night of Hanukkah
Vitamin carefully placed by my plate
Flying home in a make-believe airplane
Because of others, I wasn't lost.

College Counselor taught me to see
My children gave me courage
Therapist helped me heal
Because of others, I have power.

Companions always there
Grandchildren call
Arms wrapped around me
Because of others, I am loved.

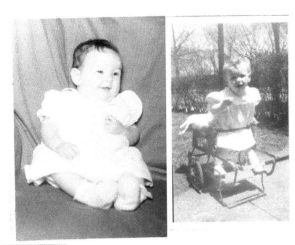

134   The Tiger in the Yard

Barbara Weber   135

About the Author

Dr. Barbara Weber obtained her Ph.D. in Educational Psychology from the University of Southern California. She has been a lifelong educator teaching elementary school, gifted pull-out, teacher continuing education, community college, and an online university. Her varied experience includes mentoring many Ph.D. candidates through the dissertation process, participating in native seminars in Toksook and Akiachak, AK, demonstrating lessons for state representatives and starring in instructional videos for educators.

Thank you so much for reading one of our **Biography / Memoirs**.
If you enjoyed our book, please check out our recommended title for your
next great read!

Z.O.S. by Kay Merkel Boruff

"...dazzling in its specificity and intensity."

–C.W. Smith, author of *Understanding Women*

Lightning Source UK Ltd.
Milton Keynes UK
UKHW020642211218
334382UK00012B/883/P